# 3 Dozen Reasons To Be An Italian
# COOKBOOK

## BY MICHAEL HANNA

**Published by Bacigalupo Publishing, LLC**

1804 Morris Street

Sarasota, FL 34239

**Production Credits**

Co-author and typesetter: Elsa Hanna

Book layout, design and photographer: Kristen Tuttle

Proofreader: Susan Tuttle

**ISBN:** 978-0-9843568-0-5

**Library of Congress Control Number:** 2009912487

Printed in the United States of America

First Edition.

# Dedication

    This book is dedicated to my mother, Florence Catherine Bacigalupo Hanna, and my son, Kenneth Michael Hanna. They both left us too early to appreciate the inspiration they instilled in me.

    My mother allowed me to understand and appreciate quality food and to finesse proper flavor from excellent Italian dishes.

    My son, namesake of my father Ken, I feel, went to Johnson and Wales University in Rhode Island because of his desire to carry on his family's tradition in the culinary arts.

# What People are Saying...

"Thanks for sharing your menu with us! What a great tasting meal we had. By eating it, my husband and myself felt to be in Italy, that's how original it was. The special combination of flavours, the pasta with the touch of garlic and a hint of herbs was just stunning!

Thanks again and good luck for all your goals and dreams!"

Beate & Peter Goldstein

Bavaria, Germany

"I want to thank you both for preparing such a wonderful meal! Sal and I really enjoyed it!

It was Chicken Marsala with mushrooms and garlic bread along with tomatoes and fresh basil in the most outrageously delicious marinade I have ever tasted! The entire meal was divine! Tender and light, completely satisfying! I thought it was absolutely great, exactly the kind of meal I hope to learn to prepare myself... someday!!

But, what do I know about Italian dishes? I'm from Colorado! I did not grow up with an Italian grandmother cooking for me. (I've only lived with Italians for the last 20 years, but that doesn't count).

So, without preamble or any introduction, I brought the meal down the street and shared it with my husband's family – that's the real test! Their reaction was very enthusiastic! These are just a few of the responses; 'scrumptious!' 'The way mamma used to make it, pure Italian,' 'better than any restaurant,' and my favorite... 'damned delicious!' I agree! Thanks for including us in the testing process; it's a rough job, but somebody's got to do it!"

Best regards,

Nanci Yarter & Sal Caputo, Proprietors

Salon Alternatives

Sarasota, FL

"Pesto – In a word… Botanically flavorful to the palate. Loved every last bite!

Thanks for indulging me!!"

Lori Frailing, O.T./C.H.T.

Sarasota, FL

☆ "Your tomato sauce (Marinara Sauce) recipe is 'absolutely delicious.' I was a little skeptical when I saw anchovies, but tried it anyway and have been making it ever since!

'The best sauce I ever ate' said my 23 yr. old son, whom also loves to cook.

My husband can't leave the kitchen once the 'wonderful aroma' reaches those Italian nostrils. He's constantly testing the sauce.

I triple the recipe because I like enough to freeze. So far I have tried it over ravioli, stuffed shells and in a meatless lasagna. All outstandingly delicious. I also added meatballs to it, to serve with my meatless lasagna.

I have to say, 'This is the best sauce recipe' I have ever made and oh, 'the aroma.'

My dad loves to come to dinner when I serve this meal.

Thank you so much for sharing!"

Nancy Bozyczko

Hopkinton, MA

"Chicken (Cacciatore) was moist and tender. All the seasonings were blended perfectly to make a very flavorful dish, giving you a wonderful taste of Italy."

Linda Loria Ericson

Sarasota, FL

Mama Filomena (Loria) says, "Molto Buono!" "

"Yummy!! Everything was <u>delicious</u>. Thank you for thinking of me."

Pat Tellbuescher

Sarasota, FL

"Thank you so much for that taste of Italy you made me. . . I am so fussy about Italian food. If you opened a restaurant, I would be a weekly patron. That Chicken Parmesan was the best I have ever tasted!"

Thanks again,

Theresa Nemeth

Sarasota, FL

"Your pasta was absolutely delicious. Excellent taste and the spices were just right. I would recommend it to anyone."

Matt Somerville

Sarasota, FL

"I had the pleasure of enjoying a wonderful dish made by Mr. Michael Hanna. He made Shrimp and Scallops with noodles in an Alfredo Sauce.

The seafood was done perfectly, tender, and succulent. The noodles were done *al dente*, just as I like them. The Alfredo sauce was flavorful, with just a hint of garlic and very smooth and creamy."

"I would certainly have this dish again. I enjoyed it very much."

Judy Lafreniere

Sarasota, FL

"Thank you so much for letting me taste two of your pasta dishes! They both were so tasty and flavorful, I didn't want to stop! The scallops and shrimp pesto was my favorite, but the pasta (Amatriciana Sauce with sausages) you gave me . . . was also, oh, so good! You're a wonderful chef!"

Marlene Kirchner

Sarasota, FL

"I got a taste of the pasta meal and it was very delicious. The pasta itself was cooked to perfection and the sauce (Marinara Sauce) was awesome. I never had anything like it, and not to mention, the garlic bread was great too. I would recommend that dish to everyone who enjoys food."

Latasha Bell

Sarasota, FL

". . . I had two of your dishes. I had the spaghetti which was wonderful. The sauce was just right. Then I had the chicken cacciatore. This was also very good. The chicken was excellent. My favorite part was the garlic bread. The bread was chewy and it had just the right amount of garlic and cheese."

Thanks,

Rachel Knepp

Sarasota, FL

"Your shrimp and scallops in pesto tossed with pasta entrée was fabulous! This is a 'gotta have' recipe. I can't wait to make it myself. Thank you for sharing such a wonderful treat."

Julie Reiter

Sarasota, FL

"I enjoyed pasta you gave me once to try. The taste was really delicious and I could hardly stop eating. Frankly speaking, that was one of the best pastas I've ever tried. And I really enjoyed olive (garlic) bread that came along with the pasta."

"It was really unforgettable experience! Thank you!"

Sincerely,

Julia Kalinina

Khabarousk, Russia

"Michael Hanna me trajo una deliciosa comida de camarones y scallops combinado con unos espaguetis y salsa de pesto. Tenia un sabor a ajo esquisito, yo creo que es la mejor comida italiana que he probado en un largo tiempo, tu debes de tratarlo, es la mejor."

Gracias,

Mabel Aliaga

Sarasota, FL

Translation: "Michael Hanna brought me a delicious meal of shrimp and scallops combined with spaghetti and pesto sauce. It had a garlic flavor that was exquisite; I think it was the best Italian meal that I have tasted in a long time. You should try it, it's the best."

# Foreword

After completing high school in 1959, I went to Europe to study art. In order to have some extra money, I found myself working at several Italian restaurants. My mother's maiden name was Florence Catherine Bacigalupo; the seeds had already been planted. When I returned home, I immediately began working at my father's restaurant, Ken's Steak House, where I designed the menu and was chef of "The Finale Room." After a few years, I joined a partnership with my family and opened "Ristorante La Bimba."

My mother, Florence Hanna, was a warm and wonderful person. She was very talented in many ways. She was a songwriter, and she was exceptional in the kitchen. Often, I recall her in the kitchen singing and cooking at the same time.

In our home town, Framingham, Massachusetts, my parents, Ken Hanna and Florence Bacigalupo Hanna, started a restaurant that I believe was called the 41 Café. But with my dad always out front and having what the Irish call "The Gift," the restaurant, by popular demand, became Ken's. As it enlarged and grew, it became Ken's Steak House. My mother started serving a salad with the steak and potato meals. The salad became so popular; people were always getting refills. After years of fame, Ken's Steak House was nationally famous for great steaks and great salads. Eventually, my father and mother started a salad dressing company with Frank and Louise Crowley, two customers who became good friends and finally partners in Ken's Foods, Inc. The original dressing of my mother's, as I remember it, became known as Ken's Italian Dressing and finally as Ken's Steak House Italian Dressing. Some nights as the family assembled for dinner, my mother would serve the meal; and then over dessert ask, "Michael, who do you think made this dressing?" "Was it me, or the company?" It was always so good; I'm not sure there was a difference.

My recipes are mine. Therefore, they are sometimes unique in order to achieve a desired flavor. The ingredients are a choice all my own. Taste my two favorites, Marinara Sauce and Béchamel Sauce, neither of which are conventional, and see for yourself. These recipes are the backbone of quite a few items.

I have a particular method of utilizing the whole garlic as well as the whole onion. In many of my recipes, I start out by heating a sauté pan. Then I crush the garlic clove and immediately place the garlic skin into the heated pan so that the juices and oils are absorbed into the particular dish that I am making. I utilize onions in a very similar manner. When onions are part of a recipe, I cut off the top and bottom portions of the onion and place them into the hot pan with the onion side down. This method also enhances the flavor of the dish that I am making.

Whenever possible, I strongly recommend that you cook pasta with bottled water. Tap water is usually influenced by local water systems as well as the environment, which can alter adversely the taste of the sauce that you are using. Bottled water is chemical free; therefore, you have more control over the outcome of your recipe.

Stove tops and ovens vary in temperature. The burners or the oven or even the broiler vary. So, as you cook, watch and adjust your burners and oven as needed. Dishes, as they become ready, start to make a sound similar to hissing. This sound comes from the evaporation in sauces as you complete the cooking of the main dish. Coordinate the preparation of the side dishes so everything is ready at once. Keep in mind that it takes about 15-20 minutes to boil water. The cooking time, on average, for pasta is about 8-10 minutes, and the boiling and cooking time for vegetables is about the same due to the size of the pan being used and the amount of water. Sautéed vegetables can even be quicker.

The Italian food was first for me. I felt Italian cooking to be the food. From Marco Polo until now, the ability of Italians to make items taste good made them the forerunners of fine cuisine. For example, Northern Italian farmers have always had sausage after dressing out pigs for market. Pancetta always salted and stored with the sausages are some of the ingredients left for the "house." As a result, "Bel Paese Pasta" is a wonderful recipe, very real to Italian homes. Fish and poultry are often used because of availability.

The knowing what goes with what has given me the direction and license to prepare food as I do. For this reason, I am emphasizing basic sauces that can be blended with so much of fish and poultry. Marinara goes very well with chicken, pork, sausage, pancetta, shrimp, scallops, cod, and swordfish. Marinara with pancetta becomes Amatriciana. Béchamel, with pasta boiled in Chicken Stock, becomes Alfredo. Marinara with Pesto is wonderful. Marinara with Béchamel becomes Red Devil. Béchamel with Pesto is out of this world. Béchamel with pancetta is a form of Carbonara. Scrod in Marinara with Pesto is Pesce Genovese. As you read my recipes, look for ideas and add-ons at the bottom of the page. All recipes are complete. The add-ons are just additional, if desired. To better understand the blending, take a tablespoon half full of the sauces you wish to mix and taste them. Pesto spread on garlic bread is very tasty. Pesto spread on swordfish or scrod or sautéed with scallops and shrimp is absolutely mouth watering. Sun-dried tomatoes sautéed with Pesto or Béchamel – even all three together – is an excellent dish. Once you have the basics, you can combine a little something with one or two other recipe items, and, "voila," you have a meal. Italian cooking – to me – is combining things that belong.

For approximately forty years, I have been perfecting Italian recipes from restaurant to family portions. Quite often I have been asked for cooking advice and to share my recipes. For more than 10 years, my wife, Elsa, has been saying, "Write it down." Finally I have, and here are the results.

I've explained the preparation in sequence in order to achieve the best results. If there is any item that is not clear to you, please write me and I'll do my best to clarify it.

Enjoy the cooking. All recipes are made with high-quality, wholesome ingredients, and I consider them healthy.

Being able to cook is very satisfying for the joy of accomplishment, the capability of knowledgeable conversation, and, finally, enjoying its consumption.

Take your time. And, I highly recommend that you attempt the Chicken Stock and then the Marinara Sauce. These two items are the basis of many of my recipes.

Please enjoy my book. Hopefully, in the future, there will be another with many more recipes. If you make this first book a part of your cooking cuisine, the second book will be even more fun.

# Contents

This chef's hat symbol let's you know Chef Michael is making special suggestions!

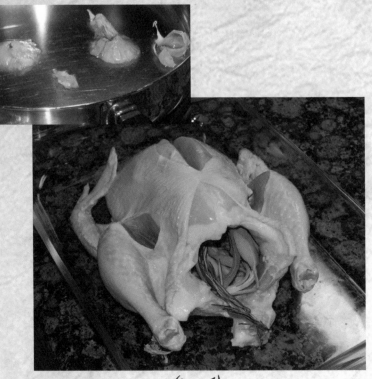

*(page 1)*

*(page 1)*

*(page 1)*

*(page 1)*

*(page 1)*

*(page 3)*

*(page 3)*

*(page 33)*

*(page 7)*

*(page 7)*

*(page 11)*

*(page 11)*

*(page 11)*

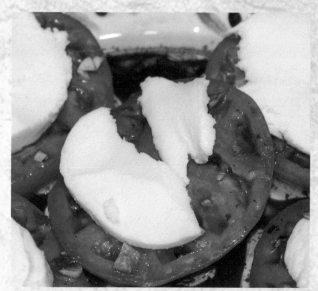

*(page 21-🍳)*

*(page 69; page 21-🍳; page 29)*

*(page 25)*

*(page 26)*

*(page 26)*

*(page 28)*

*(page 28)*

*(page 29)*

*(page 29)*

*(page 31)*

*(page 43)*

*(page 43)*

*(page 43)*

*(page 69 )*

*(page 69; page 21-* 👨‍🍳 *; page 29 )*

*(page 74)*

*(page 74)*

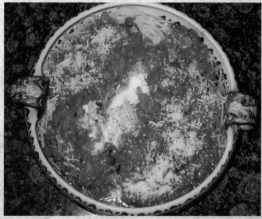

*(page 77)*

# *Foundations*
## *Roasted Chicken*
## With Rosemary Drumstick and Thighs

3 ½ lb. whole chickens (approximate weight)

4 drumsticks

4 chicken thighs

1 small and 1 medium garlic cloves

3-4 celery stalks

3 whole carrots (unpeeled)

1 medium yellow onion

4 sprigs fresh rosemary

6-8 fresh sage leaves

2 tablespoons olive oil

Black pepper

Salt (sea)

The bones/carcass from the roasted chicken and chicken parts (neck, extra drumsticks and thighs) are to be used to make Chicken Stock (see recipe).

Preheat oven to 400 degrees.

Take the whole chicken and remove any chicken parts that are usually stuffed inside of the chicken (for example: gizzards, heart). These chicken parts, except for the neck, will not be used in this recipe. Take the chicken and cut the breast down the center, and, also, cut the drumsticks and wings (do not cut these parts off of the chicken, simply slice into them). Do not cut the extra drumsticks and thighs. Chop the neck a couple of times and cook along with the chicken.

Use a roasting pan that is large enough to fit the whole chicken and the chicken parts. Crush the medium garlic clove and place it in the large roasting pan together with the garlic skin. Place the whole chicken into the large roasting pan. Take 1 tablespoon of olive oil, ¼ teaspoon of salt and ¼ teaspoon of black pepper and rub the entire chicken. Take 1 entire sprig of fresh rosemary and 2-3 sage leaves and (without chopping) stuff them into the cavity of the whole chicken. Take celery stalks and carrots and cut lengthwise and then across a couple of times (pieces should remain on the larger side). Take the pieces of celery and carrots and place some underneath the chicken, inside the chicken and in and around the legs and wings. Cut 4 slices (about ¼ inch each) from the onion and scatter the onion rings (onion skins included) underneath the chicken and inside the chicken.

Crush the small garlic; remove the garlic skin and add it to the roasting pan. Mince the garlic and mix it with some salt and black pepper and 1 tablespoon of olive oil. Take the 4 drumsticks and 4 thighs and rub them with this mixture. Place these pieces of chicken in the roasting pan with the whole chicken. Celery, carrots and onions should also be distributed onto these pieces. Take the remaining rosemary leaves and remove the leaves from their stems. Roughly chop the rosemary leaves together with the rest of the sage leaves and sprinkle them onto the whole chicken and chicken parts.

Place the roasting pan with the whole chicken and chicken parts into the oven at 400 degrees for 1 hour and 20 minutes. Half way through the cooking process, flip the chicken parts.

Once done, carve the meat from the chicken and serve, leaving the bones and carcass to be used to make Chicken Stock (see recipe).

# Chicken Stock

## Yield: 8-9 quarts

Bones/carcass from whole chicken (Roasted Chicken recipe)

Bones from chicken parts
(drumsticks and thighs from Roasted Chicken recipe)

2 small yellow onions

1 medium garlic clove

2 whole carrots (unpeeled)

2 celery stalks

8-9 quart-size containers with tight lids

Preheat oven to bake at 400 degrees.

Use the bones/carcass from the whole chicken and chicken parts (extra drumsticks and thighs) from the "Roasted Chicken with Rosemary Drumstick and Thighs" recipe. With a French knife, halve all bones, including the neck and the extra drumsticks and thighs, and chop the chicken carcass in several places, at least 4 times, and place them into a large roasting pan. Roughly chop the onions (do not discard the tops and bottoms), garlic clove (skin included), carrots, and celery stalks, and add to the roasting pan (including the onion tops and bottoms) distributing them around the carcass and bones. Place the roasting pan with all of the ingredients into the oven at 400 degrees for 1 ½ hours. Make sure that everything is cooked well but not burnt, and then remove the roasting pan from the oven.

Fill a stock pot (about 12 quart size) with 9 quarts of water. Add cooked ingredients from the roasting pan into the water in the stock pot. Once you have removed all of the ingredients from the roasting pan, place the pan on the stove top and add 1 cup of water and deglaze at medium-low heat by using a whisk to get all of the remnants from the roasting pan. Add these remnants and liquid to the stock pot of water with the other chicken ingredients. Cook the ingredients at medium heat for the first 25 minutes; then, decrease the heat to low heat for the remainder of cooking time which is 3 ½ - 4 hours. Cook uncovered.

Remove the liquid by using a ladle and then fill the quart size containers up to ½ inch from the top. Once you are finished ladling out as much liquid as possible, and if you wish to get the most out of the chicken stock, take another pot and, using a strainer, strain the ingredients. This portion could yield another quart. This recipe should yield about 8-9 quarts of fresh chicken stock. Let cool, tightly close the lids on the containers, and refrigerate or freeze. During the refrigeration or freezing process, the chicken stock will form a layer of fat on the top. Before using, skim the fat from the top of the chicken stock.

The Chicken Stock can make delicious chicken soup by adding cooked rice, carrots, and basil. Also, add salt and pepper to satisfy your personal taste.

# Personal Notes

# How to Cook Pasta

In a large pot, add water to fill about ⅓ of the pot. Cook at medium-high heat. Bring the water to a boil and then add a heavy pinch of salt and 1 teaspoon of olive oil. Stir and bring the water to a boil again. At this point, add the pasta (1 lb. will serve 4 easily) by fanning it around the pot. After one minute, stir the pasta into the water so that the pasta doesn't stick.

Total cooking time:

Fettuccine – 7-8 minutes

Linguini – 7 minutes

Spaghetti – 6 minutes

Thin Spaghetti – 5 ½ minutes

Ziti – 8 minutes

Rigatoni – 8 ½ minutes

When the pasta is done, pour about 2 tablespoons of cooking water from the pot into a serving bowl. Drain the pasta into a colander and then add pasta to the serving bowl and mix.

# Béchamel Sauce

## 2 Servings

½ pint of heavy cream

½ lb. linguini pasta

1 small garlic clove

1 tablespoon Chicken Stock (see recipe)

1 egg yolk

Fresh nutmeg

2 heaping tablespoons freshly grated fontina cheese

1 heaping tablespoon grated parmesan cheese

1 tablespoon plus 1 teaspoon olive oil

1 tablespoon butter (unsalted)

Black pepper

Salt (sea) (heavy pinch)

In a large pot, add water to fill about ⅓ of the pot. Cook at medium-high heat. Bring the water to a boil and then add a heavy pinch of salt and 1 teaspoon of olive oil. Stir and bring the water to a boil again.

While the water for the pasta is coming to a boil, crush garlic clove. Remove the garlic skin, and place the garlic skin into a large sauté pan with 1 tablespoon of olive oil and butter. Cook at low heat for about 2 minutes until the oil gets hot. Once the oil and butter get hot, remove the garlic skin and discard.

When the water in the large pot comes to a boil for the second time, add the linguini by fanning it around the pot. After 1 minute, stir the pasta into the water so that the pasta doesn't stick. Cook the linguini for a total of 7 minutes.

Add the heavy cream to the sauté pan, 3 shakes of black pepper and 5 grates of fresh nutmeg, and whisk for 2 minutes and continue to cook at low heat. Add grated fontina cheese into the cream mixture in the sauté pan, and whisk until the cheese melts, about 3 minutes. Finely mince the garlic clove and set aside. Add the chicken stock and minced garlic to the sauté pan and mix with whisk. Reduce heat slightly and simmer for 1 minute and then stir with whisk several times by moving in a circular motion around the sauté pan until the sauce reduces (slightly thickens – syrupy).

When the pasta is done, pour about 2 tablespoons of cooking water from the pot into a serving bowl. Drain the pasta into a colander and then add pasta to the serving bowl and mix.

Once the mixture in the sauté pan reduces, add the pasta with grated parmesan cheese and mix. Then, add the egg yolk on top of the pasta and mix into pasta. Serve immediately.

This sauce can be enhanced several ways by adding different ingredients at the time you add in the chicken stock and minced garlic. One way is by adding 6-8 chopped sun-dried tomatoes and/or 4 chopped fresh basil leaves. Another way is by removing the casing from 2 sweet sausages; cutting each sausage into about 8 pieces and cooking them in a sauté pan with a little bit of olive oil for about 10 minutes at low heat; then, add them to the sauce. Or, take 2 thick slices of pancetta (¼ inch thick), cut each slice into about 16 pieces, add 5 grates of fresh nutmeg, and cook in a sauté pan with a little bit of olive oil at low heat for about 10 minutes. Then, add it to the sauce.

# Personal Notes

# Pesto Sauce

## Yield: 1 cup

4 oz. fresh basil leaves

2 tablespoons pine nuts

1 large garlic clove

4 oz. grated parmesan cheese

Olive oil (a little more than 4 oz.)

Crush the garlic clove; remove the garlic skin, and place the garlic skin into a small sauté pan with a drop of olive oil. Cook at low heat for about 30 seconds until the oil gets hot. Once the oil gets hot, remove the garlic skin and discard. Immediately, add the crushed garlic and pine nuts and roast the pine nuts, turning often, for about 3 minutes until the pine nuts get some color on them.

Clean the basil leaves by removing the stems. In a blender, add the basil leaves, roasted pine nuts, crushed garlic, 2 oz. of parmesan cheese, 3 oz. of olive oil and mix at low-medium speed (it is preferable to use the "pulse" switch on your blender). Mix the ingredients well, but do not allow the mixture to become liquid. Remove the mixture from the blender and, depending on the consistency of the mixture, add an additional 1 oz. of olive oil and 2 oz. of parmesan cheese and mix. The mixture should be thick and moist, not watery.

This sauce can be mixed with Marinara Sauce and Béchamel Sauce (see recipes). Add 1 teaspoon of Pesto Sauce (see recipe) to 1 cup of Marinara Sauce or Béchamel Sauce.

# Marinara Sauce

## My Mother's Favorite

### Yield: 2 quarts

1 can of tomato sauce (large, about. 29 oz.)

1 medium garlic clove

1 small whole carrot (peeled)

1 celery stalk

1 small yellow onion

1 anchovy (flat fillet)

1 tablespoon butter (unsalted)

1 splash dry white wine

8 fresh tarragon leaves

3 oz. Chicken Stock (see recipe)

2 tablespoons olive oil

Black pepper (pinch)

Crush the garlic clove; remove the garlic skin, and place the garlic skin into a large sauté pan with the olive oil. Cut off the top and bottom portions of the onion, and place them into the sauté pan with the onion side down and cook at low heat for about 2 minutes until the oil gets hot. Once the oil gets hot, remove the garlic skin and top and bottom portions of the onion and discard.

Cut and chop celery stalk and carrot and dice the onion and add them to the sauté pan with butter. Continue to cook at low heat and cook until onions are transparent in color.

Mince the garlic clove together with anchovy fillet and add them to the sauté pan. Chop the tarragon leaves after removing the stems. Once the onions are transparent, add one pinch of black pepper and a splash of white wine and a can of tomato sauce and chopped tarragon and increase the heat to medium. Pour the chicken stock into the empty tomato sauce can. Swirl the chicken stock around the empty can to collect any tomato sauce residue; then, pour the chicken stock together with the residue into the sauté pan. Mix the ingredients and cook for 8-10 minutes; then reduce to medium-low heat and cook for 45 minutes.

For extra flavor, you can add 3-6 (depending on personal taste) chopped leaves of fresh basil (roll the basil leaves and cut) at the time that you add the chopped tarragon. Another flavorful suggestion is to add either 1 teaspoon of Pesto Sauce (see recipe) or 1 tablespoon of Béchamel Sauce (see recipe) or both to 1 cup of Marinara Sauce.

# Appetizers

## Caesar's Salad Dressing

### 3-4 Servings

¾ head romaine lettuce

1 egg

2 anchovies (flat fillet)

1 small garlic clove

1 tablespoon worcestershire sauce

½ cup olive oil

1 tablespoon red wine vinegar

1 fork load dijon mustard

Juice from ¼ - ½ fresh lemon

⅛ teaspoon black pepper

Croutons

Parmesan cheese

Remove the leaves from the romaine lettuce, and rinse each leaf with cool water. To dry the lettuce leaves, place the leaves next to each other on top of a row of clean, white paper towels. Continue to layer the paper towels and leaves until you have all of the leaves on top of towels. Place another row of paper towels on top of the top layer of leaves; then, roll the entire bunch. It is very important to dry the lettuce leaves as much as possible because the water will dilute the dressing. Set this aside.

Place the egg in a small bowl of hot water (hot water from the tap) and let sit. If you have a mortar and pestle, they are great tools to use to grind and mix the garlic, anchovy, and black pepper. Finely mince garlic clove together with anchovy fillets and, if you do not have a mortar and pestle, use the back of a tablespoon to grind the garlic and anchovy into a paste together with ⅛ teaspoon of black pepper. Place the garlic, anchovy, and black pepper paste in a large salad bowl (preferably glass).

Add the juice from ¼ - ½ of a fresh lemon and the dijon mustard. Then, add red wine vinegar, worcestershire sauce, and olive oil. Gently mix with a whisk. Crack and add the raw egg and whisk the entire mixture vigorously to make it slightly thick. Remove the dressing from the bowl, but do not clean the bowl if you are going to use the bowl to mix the salad.

Remove the lettuce leaves from the paper towels, and tear up the lettuce and add to the salad bowl. Add the dressing a little at a time and toss. Check the consistency of the dressing on the lettuce. The lettuce should be covered but not saturated.

Add parmesan cheese to obtain a desired flavor. Add some croutons and toss the entire salad. Serve immediately.

This dressing can be made in advance and put into the refrigerator for a couple of hours. In fact, the cooling seems to make it coagulate a little, which gives the salad a more robust flavor. Of all the Caesar's Salads I have tasted, this, by far, is my favorite and, coincidentally, it's my wife, Elsa's, recipe.

# Personal Notes

# Tossed Salad

## 2 Servings

½ head lettuce (preferably bib or Boston leaf lettuce)

2 tablespoons olive oil

2 tablespoons red wine vinegar

2 slices from a medium yellow onion

2 slices from a medium tomato

1 tablespoon grated parmesan cheese

1 small garlic clove

Black pepper (2 pinches)

Salt (sea) (2 pinches)

Crush garlic clove; rub a piece of crushed garlic around the inside of a large salad bowl. Add olive oil and swirl the oil around the bowl to spread the oil. Add the black pepper and salt by sprinkling them around the bowl. Cut and chop 2 slices from a medium onion and 2 slices from a medium tomato and add them to the bowl. Add the red wine vinegar.

Remove the leaves of ½ head of bib or Boston leaf lettuce, clean the leaves with cool water, and pat dry with a clean, white paper towel. Add the leaves (tear if necessary) to the salad bowl and toss. Sprinkle the parmesan cheese and mix.

# Antipasto

## 4 Servings

1 head romaine lettuce

6 cooked jumbo shrimp (about ¼ lb.)

6 oz. can of solid white albacore tuna

8 slices sopressata salami

4 oz. turkey breast slices

6 slices American cheese

1 medium garlic clove

½ medium yellow onion

3 tablespoons olive oil

2 tablespoons balsamic vinegar

1 tablespoon red wine vinegar

2 tablespoons shredded parmesan cheese

⅛ teaspoon black pepper

Salt (sea) (generous pinch)

Crush garlic clove; rub a piece of crushed garlic around the inside of a large salad bowl. Add 2 tablespoons of olive oil, 1 tablespoon of balsamic vinegar, and red wine vinegar to the salad bowl and swirl the ingredients around the bowl. Chop and dice the onion and add. Sprinkle the salt and black pepper into the bowl.

Open the can of solid white albacore tuna and drain the juice and rinse the tuna by adding water and draining the water out by squeezing the top of the can onto the tuna; then, add the tuna to the salad bowl. Remove the tails from the shrimp and make sure that they are clean and deveined and add to the bowl. Mix the tuna fish and shrimp into the salad dressing mixture.

Take the cold cuts and cut them in half and then cut into slices. Layer the cold cuts on top of the ingredients already in the bowl. Drizzle 1 tablespoon of balsamic vinegar and 1 tablespoon of olive oil on top. Wash the romaine lettuce by rinsing the individual leaves with cool water. Pat dry the leaves with clean, white paper towels. Tear the romaine lettuce into pieces and add them to the salad bowl on top of the ingredients. Before mixing, add parmesan cheese. Mix the salad and, at the same time, separate the cold cuts and the rest of the ingredients.

Optional Ingredients: Olives, pepperoncinis, marinated mushrooms, artichoke hearts, ham, mortadella

# Minestrone Soup

## Yield: 8 quarts

1 medium garlic clove

2 -3 slices prosciutto di Parma

2 medium yellow onions

2 celery stalks

2 whole carrots

½ head cabbage

½ lb. cauliflower

1-2 yellow (summer) squash (depending on size)

¼ lb. green beans

1 can cannellini beans

1 can red kidney beans

10 cups Chicken Stock (see recipe)

4 oz. elbow macaroni

2 anchovies (flat fillet)

Olive oil (a little more than 4 tablespoons)

Black pepper (generous pinch)

Salt (sea) (pinch)

Crush garlic clove; remove the garlic skin, and place the garlic skin into a large pot with 4 tablespoons of olive oil. Cut off the top and bottom portions of the onions and place them into the large pot with the onion side down and cook at low heat for about 2 minutes until the oil gets hot. Once the oil gets hot, remove the garlic skin and top and bottom portions of the onions and discard.

Finely chop the prosciutto di Parma and add to the pot together with a generous pinch of black pepper and cook at medium-low heat until the prosciutto gets color, about 3-4 minutes. Cut and finely chop the celery stalks, whole carrot, onions, and cabbage and add all of these ingredients into the pot. Cook these ingredients for 5 minutes at medium-low heat. Finely mince the garlic clove together with the anchovy fillets and add to the pot. Slice the squash, cut the cauliflower, and clean and chop the green beans (remove the tips and chop into thirds or quarters) and add to the pot with the rest of the ingredients and cook for an additional 5 minutes. While the ingredients in the pot are cooking, open the can of cannellini and kidney beans and drain and rinse the beans with fresh water and add to pot. Add chicken stock and 10 cups of water (preferably bottled) and stir all of the ingredients and cook at medium heat until it comes to a boil.

In a small sauce pan, add 8 oz. of water, a pinch of salt, and a couple of drops of olive oil. Bring the water to a boil and add the elbow macaroni. Partially cook the macaroni for 3 minutes; then drain and add to the large pot and stir.

Bring the soup to a boil, and let the soup boil for 10 minutes; then, simmer the soup (uncovered) at just above low heat for a minimum of one hour.

In addition to the macaroni, potatoes can be added to this soup just before the beans are added. Begin preparing the potatoes at the beginning of the recipe. Take 6 small red potatoes and wash them by placing them in a colander and rinsing them with cool water. In a small pot, add water to fill about ½ of the pot (enough to cover 6 small red potatoes). Bring the water to a boil, add a pinch of salt, add the potatoes, and boil at medium heat for 25 minutes. Remove the potatoes and place them on a cutting board. Pat dry all of the potatoes using clean, white paper towels. Let the potatoes cool for 20 minutes. Once the potatoes are cool, cut the smaller potatoes in half and the larger ones in quarters.

# Vegetables
## Marinated Steak House Tomatoes

### 3-4 Servings

1 beefy steak house tomato

1 medium garlic clove

1 tablespoon balsamic vinegar

1 tablespoon red wine vinegar

6 fresh oregano leaves

3 tablespoons olive oil

Black pepper

Salt (sea)

Slice the tomato into about 5 pieces (about ¼ inch thick) by placing the tomato on its side and slicing and setting aside. In a deep dish, add the olive oil. Finely mince garlic clove and add to the dish together with balsamic vinegar and red wine vinegar. Chop oregano leaves and add and mix well. Then, place the tomato slices into the marinade and let them sit for a few minutes; next, turn the tomatoes over and lightly sprinkle each tomato with black pepper and salt.

Refrigerate before serving.

The marinated tomatoes can be enhanced even further by adding mozzarella cheese. Take a fresh (ball) of mozzarella cheese (whole milk) and cut 5 thick slices (about ¼ inch thick) and place one slice on top of each slice of tomato.

# Spinach Stuffing

## Yield: 2 cups

1 small box frozen spinach (plain)

1 small garlic clove

1 small yellow onion

Ritz crackers (one roll)

8 oz. grated cheddar cheese

2 tablespoons grated parmesan cheese

1 egg yolk

½ tablespoon olive oil

Fresh nutmeg

Black pepper

Thaw out the frozen spinach and drain by squeezing as much moisture out as possible before setting aside. Finely mince the garlic clove and dice and chop the onion and set aside. Grate the cheddar cheese and set aside.

In a sauté pan add olive oil, the drained spinach, minced garlic and chopped onion and cook at low heat until the onions become transparent, about 6 minutes.

In a separate bowl, add finely crushed roll of Ritz crackers together with 2 pinches of black pepper, 4-5 grates of fresh nutmeg, grated cheddar cheese, and grated parmesan cheese and mix well.

Remove the ingredients from the sauté pan and add to the mixture in the bowl and mix. Add egg yolk to the mixture and mix well. Add more black pepper and nutmeg if you feel it needs a little bit more flavor.

# Sautéed Vegetables: Summer Squash and Plum Tomatoes

## 2 Servings

4 plum tomatoes

1 small yellow onion

1 medium garlic clove

1 summer (yellow) squash (or zucchini)

1 tablespoon balsamic vinegar

1 tablespoon red wine vinegar

2 tablespoons olive oil

1 tablespoon butter (unsalted)

Black pepper

Salt (sea)

Cut the tomatoes in half and then quarter. Take each piece and cut into 4 pieces making about 16 pieces from one tomato. Cut the summer squash in half lengthwise and then cut it into about 20 pieces. Cut and chop one slice of onion. Finely mince ½ of the garlic clove.

Add the tomatoes, summer squash, chopped onion, minced garlic, olive oil, butter, balsamic vinegar, red wine vinegar with two pinches of black pepper and a pinch of salt into a small sauté pan and cook at medium-low heat for 5 minutes. Stir the ingredients; then reduce the heat to low and continue to cook for another 2 minutes. Serve immediately.

To enhance the flavor of the vegetables, sprinkle them with parmesan cheese.

# Green Beans

## 2 Servings

20 green beans

1 tablespoon butter (unsalted)

1 tablespoon balsamic vinegar

1 tablespoon olive oil

Black pepper

Salt (sea)

Grab the green beans in one bunch and cut the tips off at one end. Turn the entire bunch around and cut the tips off of the opposite end.

In a small sauce pan (wide enough so that the green beans can lay flat) add butter and cook at low heat. Once the butter begins to bubble, add olive oil, a pinch of black pepper, a pinch of salt, and balsamic vinegar. Add the beans to the sauce pan and cook for 5 minutes. When serving the beans, add some balsamic vinegar mixture on top.

If you are making the green beans to accompany the Chicken Saltimbocca (see recipe) dish, add the beans to the baking dish with the chicken and bake in the oven with the Chicken Saltimbocca for 5 minutes. Save the balsamic vinegar mixture to put on the green beans prior to serving.

# Garlic and Spinach

## 2 Servings

9-10 oz. fresh spinach

1 small garlic clove

1 tablespoon butter (unsalted)

1 tablespoon olive oil

Black pepper

Salt (sea)

Crush garlic clove; remove the garlic skin, and place the garlic skin into a sauté pan with olive oil and cook at low heat for about 2 minutes until the oil gets hot. Once the oil gets hot, remove the garlic skin and discard.

Clean the fresh spinach by removing the stems and deveining the leaves. Finely mince the garlic clove. Add the minced garlic, cleaned spinach, a generous pinch of salt, a generous pinch of black pepper, and butter to the sauté pan and sauté the spinach at low heat for 4 minutes, constantly turning the spinach. Serve immediately.

To devein a fresh spinach leaf, take the leaf and place it face down, then pinch the back ridge of the leaf and pull the "vein" away from the leaf.

# Marinated Asparagus

## 4-6 Servings

1 bunch fresh baby asparagus
(preferably thin, slim; about 1 lb.)

1 small garlic clove

1 tablespoon balsamic vinegar

2 tablespoons olive oil

Black pepper

Salt (sea)


Take the baby asparagus and cut ¼ inch off the bottom of each stalk.  (If the asparagus are large, then cut ¼ inch off the bottom of each stalk and boil in water at medium heat for 4-5 minutes.)  Finely mince garlic clove and set aside.  In a deep dish, add the minced garlic, olive oil, balsamic vinegar, 2 pinches of salt, and 2 pinches of black pepper and mix well.

Lay all of the asparagus flat and roll them around so that all areas of the asparagus gets saturated with the mixture.  Cover and refrigerate for a minimum of 4 hours. This can be done the day before and kept refrigerated until it is ready to be served.

# Personal Notes

# Roast Potatoes Rosemary

## 4 Servings

12 red potatoes (small-medium)

4 sprigs fresh rosemary

1 medium or 2 small garlic cloves

3 tablespoons olive oil

½ teaspoon black pepper

½ teaspoon salt (sea)

Wash the potatoes by placing them in a colander and rinsing them with cool water. In a small pot, add water to fill ½ of the pot and add a pinch of salt. Bring the water to a boil and then add the potatoes (unpeeled) to the boiling water. Boil the potatoes at medium heat for 25 minutes. Remove the potatoes and place them on a cutting board. Pat dry all of the potatoes using clean, white paper towels. Let the potatoes cool for 20 minutes. Once the potatoes are cool, cut the smaller potatoes in half and the larger ones in quarters.

Finely mince garlic clove(s) and set aside. In a baking dish, add olive oil, salt, black pepper, and minced garlic. Remove the rosemary leaves from their stem, chop the rosemary leaves, and add them to the baking dish and mix with the other ingredients. Add all of the potatoes into the baking dish by placing them open faced down into the oil and rosemary mixture. Spoon the oil and rosemary mixture onto all sides of the potatoes. Cover the baking dish and place it into the refrigerator for at least 1 hour.

When the potatoes are ready to be cooked, preheat oven to bake at 400 degrees.

Remove the baking dish with the potatoes from the refrigerator, and mix the potatoes thoroughly with the oil and rosemary mixture. Place the baking dish into the oven, and cook at 400 degrees for 40 minutes.

# Breads
## Garlic Bread

1 large baguette or Italian bread

1 medium garlic clove

¼ cup olive oil

3 tablespoon butter (unsalted)

1 long sprig fresh rosemary

¼ teaspoon black pepper

Preheat oven to bake at 400 degrees.

Cut bread into about 6 pieces and then cut each piece in half. Crush garlic clove; remove the garlic skin and place the garlic skin into a large sauté pan with olive oil and butter and cook at low heat for about 2 minutes until the oil gets hot. Once the oil gets hot, remove the garlic skin and discard.

Remove the rosemary leaves from their stem, chop the rosemary leaves, and add them to the sauté pan.

Finely mince the garlic clove and add it to the sauté pan together with black pepper. Mix and allow garlic to cook lightly for about 2-3 minutes depending on the color of the garlic (do not overcook). Take pieces of bread and dip and press each piece of bread into the pan to soak up the garlic/butter mixture. Place the pieces of bread in a baking dish with garlic/butter mixture side up. Cook in the oven for about 8-10 minutes, until golden brown (do not overcook).

To add some extra flavor, sprinkle parmesan cheese and shredded or grated mozzarella cheese on each piece of bread before baking.

# Egg and Bread

## 3-4 Servings

3 whole eggs

½ loaf of good quality French baguette or Italian bread

1 medium garlic clove

1 anchovy (flat fillet)

3 tablespoons olive oil

3 tablespoons butter (unsalted)

Black pepper

Salt (sea)

Cut bread into cubes (about ¾ inch).

Crush garlic clove; remove the garlic skin and place the garlic skin into a sauté pan with 2 tablespoons of olive oil and cook at low heat for about 2 minutes until the oil gets hot. Once the oil gets hot, remove the garlic skin and discard.

Finely mince the garlic clove together with anchovy fillet and add to the sauté pan together with 2 tablespoons of butter, 5 shakes (slightly less than ⅛ teaspoon) of black pepper, and a pinch of salt. Mix and continue to cook at low heat. When the ingredients begin to bubble, add the bread and stir constantly so that all sides absorb some of the oil and butter and get a little color on the white portions.*

Crack the eggs into a bowl. Add 4 shakes of black pepper and stir vigorously; then pour over the bread in the sauté pan. Stir bread as you are pouring the egg to evenly distribute the egg over the bread. Stir for about 45 seconds and serve.

*If needed: If bread is too dry, add an additional 1 tablespoon of oil or butter and then mix.

# Bruschetta

6 plum tomatoes

1 loaf baguette bread

1 tablespoon balsamic vinegar

½ tablespoon red wine vinegar

6-8 fresh oregano leaves (depending on size of bud)

1 medium and 1 small garlic cloves

½ anchovy (flat fillet)

1 sprig fresh rosemary

Grated parmesan cheese

4 tablespoons olive oil

1 tablespoon butter (unsalted)

Black pepper

Salt (sea)


Cut tomatoes in half and then quarter. Take each piece and cut into 4 pieces making about 16 pieces from each tomato and set aside. In a separate dish, mix 2 tablespoons of olive oil, balsamic vinegar, red wine vinegar, a good pinch of salt, and a good pinch of black pepper. Crumble fresh oregano leaves and add to the mixture. Mince one small garlic clove and add to mixture and whisk together. Add all of the tomato pieces into the mixture and mix well to make sure that all parts of the tomatoes get saturated with the mixture.

After this is mixed well, cover and refrigerate for a minimum of 2 hours.

For the bread preparation: Slice the baguette bread into 4 inch pieces; then cut each piece in half and set the pieces of bread aside. Crush 1 medium garlic clove; remove the garlic skin, and place the garlic skin into a large sauté pan with 2 tablespoons of olive oil. Cook at low heat for about 2 minutes until the oil gets hot. Once the oil gets hot, remove the garlic skin and discard.

Add butter to the sauté pan and continue to cook at low heat. Finely mince 1 medium garlic clove together with anchovy fillet and add the mixture to the sauté pan. Remove the rosemary leaves from their stem, chop the rosemary leaves, and add them to the sauté pan. Mix the ingredients in the sauté pan and bring the mixture to a boil; then, add a pinch of black pepper and mix. After one minute, dip and press each piece of bread into the pan to soak up the mixture. Place the pieces of bread in a baking dish with mixture side up. Sprinkle parmesan cheese on each piece of bread.

Preheat oven to bake at 400 degrees.

Place 4-5 pieces of chopped, marinated plum tomatoes on each piece of bread and bake for 8-10 minutes at 350 – 400 degrees. As soon as the pieces of bread begin to get color, remove them from the oven.

For extra flavor, a thin layer of Pesto Sauce (see recipe) may be applied on top of each piece of bread before adding the marinated plum tomatoes.

# Pasta
## Aglio Burro Pasta

**2 Servings**

½ lb. linguini pasta

1 medium garlic clove

10 sprigs fresh flat parsley

1 egg yolk

1 tablespoon plus 1 teaspoon olive oil

2 tablespoons butter (unsalted)

3 tablespoons grated parmesan cheese

Black pepper (heavy pinch)

Salt (sea) (heavy pinch)


In a large pot, add water to fill about ⅓ of the pot. Cook at medium-high heat. Bring the water to a boil and then add a heavy pinch of salt and 1 teaspoon of olive oil. Stir and bring the water to a boil again. At this point, add the linguini by fanning it around the pot. After one minute, stir the pasta into the water so that the pasta doesn't stick. Cook the linguini for a total of 7 minutes.

While the pasta is cooking, crush garlic clove; remove the garlic skin, and place the garlic skin into a sauté pan with 1 tablespoon of olive oil. Cook at low heat for about 2 minutes until the oil gets hot. Once the oil gets hot, remove the garlic skin and discard.

Finely, mince the garlic clove together with the parsley; then, add them to the sauté pan with a good pinch of black pepper. One minute before the pasta is done, add 1 tablespoon of butter to the sauté pan.

When the pasta is done, pour about 2 tablespoons of cooking water from the pot into a serving bowl. Drain the pasta into a colander and then add the pasta to the serving bowl and mix. Once mixed, add the pasta to the sauté pan and add an additional 1 tablespoon of butter, egg yolk, and parmesan cheese and then mix.

Serve immediately.

A very good addition to this pasta is to add 1 anchovy fillet. Mince the anchovy fillet with the garlic and parsley and add it into the sauté pan at the same time.

# Fresh Plum and Sun-Dried Tomatoes Sauce

## 2 Servings

6 plum tomatoes

8 sun-dried tomatoes

1 small garlic clove

1 medium yellow onion

1 anchovy (flat fillet)

8 fresh basil leaves

½ lb. fettuccine pasta

3-4 tablespoons grated parmesan cheese

2 tablespoons Chicken Stock (see recipe)

2 tablespoons plus 1 teaspoon olive oil

Butter (unsalted)

Black pepper

Salt (sea)

Crush garlic clove; remove the garlic skin, and place the garlic skin into a large sauté pan with 2 tablespoons of olive oil. Cut off the top and bottom portions of the onion, and place them into the sauté pan with the onion side down and cook at low heat for about 2 minutes until the oil gets hot. Once the oil gets hot, remove the garlic skin and top and bottom portions of the onion and discard.

Cut and dice 2 slices of onion. Cut plum tomatoes lengthwise into 4 pieces and then cut each piece at least a dozen times. Slice sundried tomatoes at least 4 times.

Add the chopped onions, tomatoes, and sun-dried tomatoes to the sauté pan and continue to cook at low heat turning the ingredients over every minute for 5 minutes. Add a pinch of salt and a pinch of black pepper. Cut off the stems of the basil leaves, roll the leaves up, and slice and add to the sauté pan. Add chicken stock and butter and simmer at low heat for 20 minutes.

In a large pot, add water to fill about ⅓ of the pot. Cook at medium-high heat. Bring the water to a boil and then add a heavy pinch of salt and 1 teaspoon of olive oil. Stir and bring the water to a boil again. At this point, add the fettuccine by fanning it around the pot. After one minute, stir pasta into water so that the pasta doesn't stick. Cook the fettuccine for a total of 8 minutes. When the pasta is done, pour about 2 tablespoons of cooking water from the pot into a serving bowl. Drain the pasta into a colander and then add the pasta to the serving bowl and mix.

Finely mince the garlic clove together with anchovy fillet and add to the sauté pan and continue to cook for an additional 5 minutes.

Once the mixture in the sauté pan is done, add the pasta to the sauté pan and mix well. Add parmesan cheese and mix and serve immediately.

Once the mixture in the sauté pan is done, 2 tablespoons of Béchamel Sauce (see recipe) may be added to enhance the flavor. Mix the Béchamel Sauce into the sauté pan before adding the pasta and simmer for 1-2 minutes.

# Linguini and Sausages

## 2 Servings

2 sausages (sweet)

1 ½ cups Marinara Sauce (see recipe)

½ lb. linguini pasta

1 small garlic clove

1 anchovy (flat fillet)

Parmesan cheese

2 tablespoons plus 1 teaspoon olive oil

Fresh nutmeg

Black pepper

Salt (sea)


Remove casing from sausages and cut each sausage into about 8 pieces and set aside.

Crush garlic clove; remove the garlic skin, and place the garlic skin into a large sauté pan with 2 tablespoons of olive oil and cook at low heat for about 2 minutes until the oil gets hot. Once the oil is hot, remove the garlic skin and discard.

Finely mince the garlic clove together with the anchovy fillet and add to the sauté pan. Also, add the sausage pieces, a pinch of black pepper, and 4-5 grates of fresh nutmeg. Sauté the sausage pieces at low heat by cooking the pieces for 3 minutes on each side. Once the sausage pieces are cooked, add the Marinara Sauce to the sauté pan and cook at low heat for 25 minutes.

In a large pot, add water to fill about ⅓ of the pot. Cook at medium-high heat. Bring the water to a boil and then add a heavy pinch of salt and 1 teaspoon of olive oil. Stir and bring the water to a boil again. At this point, add linguini by fanning it around the pot. After one minute, stir pasta into water so that the pasta doesn't stick. Cook the linguini for a total of 7 minutes. When the pasta is done, pour about 2 tablespoons of cooking water from the pot into a serving bowl. Drain the pasta into a colander and then add pasta to a serving bowl and mix.

Once the mixture in the sauté pan is done, add the pasta to the sauté pan with sausage and Marinara Sauce and mix. Add desired amount of parmesan cheese and serve.

This recipe may also be cooked without the Marinara Sauce. The sausages in a light sauce are very delicious.

# Carbonara Sauce with Fettuccine

## 4 Servings

1 lb. fettuccine pasta

3 slices pancetta (about ¼ inch thick)

¾ cup freshly grated asiago cheese

1 small garlic clove

1 anchovy (flat fillet)

1 egg

Fresh nutmeg

2 tablespoons plus 1 teaspoon olive oil

2 tablespoons butter (unsalted)

2 tablespoons grated parmesan cheese

Black pepper

Salt (sea) (heavy pinch)

In a large pot, add water to fill about ⅓ of the pot. Cook at medium-high heat. Bring the water to a boil and then add a heavy pinch of salt and 1 teaspoon of olive oil. Stir and bring the water to a boil again.

Crush garlic clove; remove the garlic skin, and place the garlic skin into a large sauté pan with 2 tablespoons of olive oil and cook at low heat for about 2 minutes until the oil gets got. Once the oil is hot, remove the garlic skin and discard.

Also add a generous pinch of black pepper, 5 grates of fresh nutmeg, and 2 tablespoons of butter and allow the mixture to come to a boil. Cut each slice of pancetta into about 16 pieces and add to the sauté pan. Brown the pancetta on all sides by cooking at low heat for about 10 minutes turning occasionally to make sure that all sides of the pancetta are cooked. Finely mince the garlic clove together with anchovy fillet and add to the sauté pan and continue to cook at low heat for an additional 2 minutes.

When the water in the large pot comes to a boil for the second time, add the fettuccine by fanning it around the pot. After one minute, stir pasta into water so that the pasta doesn't stick. Cook the fettuccine for a total of 7-8 minutes. When the pasta is done, pour about 2 tablespoons of cooking water from the pot into a serving bowl. Drain the pasta into a colander and then add the pasta to the serving bowl and mix.

Right before adding the pasta to the sauté pan, increase the heat to medium; then add the pasta to the sauté and mix. While mixing, add one egg yolk and continue to toss the pasta. Add grated asiago cheese and toss. To add extra flavor, add 2 tablespoons of parmesan cheese and toss and serve immediately.

This recipe can be done with either 1 egg yolk or 1 whole egg. Another variation of this recipe is to add 2 tablespoons of Béchamel Sauce (see recipe). Lightly heat the Béchamel Sauce in a small sauce pan at low heat and add to the recipe at the time and instead of the egg yolk.

# Bel Paese Pasta

## 2 Servings

2 sausages (sweet)

2 slices of pancetta (about ¼ inch thick)

½ lb. spaghetti

1 anchovy (flat fillet)

1 medium garlic clove

1 egg yolk

Fresh nutmeg

1 tablespoon butter (unsalted)

2 tablespoons plus 1 teaspoon olive oil

3 heaping tablespoons parmesan cheese

Black pepper (2 pinches)

Salt (sea) (heavy pinch)


Remove casing from sausages and cut each sausage into about 9 pieces and set aside. Cut each slice of pancetta into about 16 pieces and set aside.

Crush garlic clove; remove the garlic skin, and place the garlic skin into a sauté pan with 2 tablespoons of olive oil. Cook at low heat for about 2 minutes until the oil gets hot. Once the oil gets hot, remove the garlic skin and discard.

Finely mince the garlic clove together with anchovy fillet and set aside. Add the pancetta and sausage pieces to the sauté pan together with 5 grates of fresh nutmeg and two pinches of black pepper. Cook the sausage and pancetta at low heat for 8-10 minutes, turning the pieces over so that all sides have color.

In a large pot add water to fill about ⅓ of the pot. Cook at medium-high heat. Bring the water to a boil and then add a heavy pinch of salt and 1 teaspoon of olive oil. Stir and bring the water to a boil again. At this point, add the spaghetti by fanning it around the pot. After one minute, stir the pasta into the water so that the pasta doesn't stick. Cook the spaghetti for a total of 6 minutes. When the pasta is done, pour about 2 tablespoons of cooking water from the pot into a serving bowl. Drain the pasta into a colander and then add pasta to the serving bowl and mix.

One minute before the pasta is ready, add the minced garlic, anchovy, and butter to the sauté pan and mix. Continue to cook at low heat until the garlic gets color (do not overcook) and the butter boils. Add the pasta to sauté pan and toss several times. Add at least 2 heaping tablespoons of parmesan cheese and the egg yolk. Toss in the pan a couple of times adding 1 more tablespoon of parmesan cheese and serve immediately.

This sauce can be enriched by adding 1-2 tablespoons of Béchamel Sauce (see recipe). Lightly heat the Béchamel Sauce in a small sauce pan at low heat and add to the recipe at the time and instead of the egg yolk.

# Lasagna with Spinach Stuffing

## 12 Servings

14 lasagna noodles

8 oz. fresh (ball) mozzarella cheese (whole milk)

1 cup shredded mozzarella cheese (whole milk)
(acceptable to use packaged shredded mozzarella cheese)

1 cup freshly grated asiago cheese

Ricotta cheese (whole milk) (large container, 2 lb.)

Parmesan cheese (grated or shredded)

Spinach Stuffing (see recipe)

4 cups Marinara Sauce (see recipe)

Fresh nutmeg

1 teaspoon olive oil

Chicken Stock (see recipe)

Black pepper (pinch)

Salt (sea) (heavy pinch)

In a large pot, add water to fill about ⅓ of the pot. Cook at medium-high heat. Bring the water to a boil and then add a heavy pinch of salt and olive oil. Stir and bring the water to a boil again. At this point, add the lasagna noodles by fanning them around the pot. After one minute, stir pasta into water so that the noodles don't stick. Cook the lasagna noodles for 4-5 minutes and remove them from the water and set aside. It is advisable to put a small amount of olive oil on the noodles so that they do not stick.

If you are using freshly made Marinara Sauce, disregard the heating directions for the Marinara Sauce. If you are using leftover Marinara Sauce, then heat up the sauce by placing it in a small sauce pan at low heat for 2-3 minutes. If you are using an entire container, of Marinara Sauce, then add a small amount of Chicken Stock to the container, swirl it around to get any residue sauce from the container, and add it to the small sauce pan with the Marinara Sauce. Heat the sauce at low heat until it is warm. Remember, the sauce will be cooked in with the lasagna.

Preheat oven to bake at 400 degrees. Cut the fresh mozzarella cheese into ¼ inch thick slices (as many as you can get out of one ball) and set aside.

In a large rectangular baking dish (about 15 inches by 9 inches), put a small amount of Marinara Sauce on the bottom of the baking dish, and add one layer of noodles so that the noodles touch. If possible, place noodles so that they touch all sides of the baking dish and each other without overlapping. On the first layer, evenly spread ricotta cheese, and on top of the ricotta cheese evenly spread a few grates of nutmeg and a pinch of black pepper. Sprinkle a generous amount of asiago cheese and grated mozzarella cheese. Also, add a small amount of Marinara Sauce. Add a second layer of noodles in the same manner as the first layer. This time, evenly spread a generous amount of ricotta cheese, 5-6 grates of fresh nutmeg, a pinch of black pepper, and some Marinara Sauce. Add a third layer of noodles as previously done. On this layer, evenly spread a generous amount of Spinach Stuffing. Add a fourth and top layer of noodles as previously done. On this top layer, add a generous amount of Marinara Sauce, sprinkle asiago cheese, slices of mozzarella cheese, and sprinkle grated or shredded parmesan cheese.

Cover the baking dish with aluminum foil and cook in the oven for 30 minutes at 400 degrees. When the lasagna has cooked for 30 minutes, remove the aluminum foil and place the baking dish back into the oven and cook, uncovered, at the same 400 degrees for an additional 5 minutes.

Cut into squares about 4 inches by 3 inches and serve onto serving plates with some hot Marinara Sauce on top.

For added flavor, add 2 tablespoons of Béchamel Sauce (see recipe) on top of the spinach stuffing layer.

# Amatriciana Sauce

## 4 Servings

## Yield: 2 quarts

1 large can of tomato sauce (about 29 oz.)

1 lb. linguini pasta

2 slices pancetta (¼ inch thick each)

1 medium garlic clove

1 anchovy (flat fillet)

1 celery stalk

1 whole carrot (peeled)

1 small yellow onion

¼ cup beef broth (low sodium)

Splash of red wine (dry)

Fresh nutmeg

2 tablespoons plus 1 teaspoon olive oil

Butter (unsalted)

Black pepper

Salt (sea)

Crush garlic clove; remove the garlic skin, and place the garlic skin into a large sauté pan with 2 tablespoons of olive oil. Cut off the top and bottom portions of the onion, and place them into the sauté pan with the onion side down and cook at low heat for about 2 minutes until the oil gets hot. Once the oil gets hot, remove the garlic skin and the top and bottom portions of the onion and discard.

Finely mince garlic clove together with anchovy fillet and chop the onion. Cut the pancetta into small pieces. Cut and chop celery stalk and whole carrot, and set all of these ingredients aside.

Add the chopped pancetta into the sauté pan. In addition, add 5-6 grates of fresh nutmeg with a good pinch of black pepper. Add the chopped onion, celery and carrot pieces. Cook until celery and onions are transparent, and pancetta is brown (turning over frequently), at low heat for about 10 minutes. At this time, add the minced garlic and the anchovies.

Then, add tomato sauce to the sauté pan. Take beef broth and pour it into the empty tomato sauce can. Swirl the beef broth around to collect any tomato sauce residue; then, pour the beef broth together with the residue into the sauté pan. Add butter and a splash of dry red wine. Mix all of the ingredients and cook, uncovered, at low heat for about 50 minutes.

About 15-20 minutes before the sauce is done, begin the pasta. In a large pot, add water to fill about ⅓ of the pot. Cook at medium-high heat. Bring the water to a boil and then add a heavy pinch of salt and 1 teaspoon of olive oil. Stir and bring the water to a boil again. At this point, add the linguini by fanning it around the pot. After one minute, stir the pasta into the water so that the pasta doesn't stick. Cook the linguini for a total of 7 minutes. When the pasta is done, pour about 2 tablespoon of cooking water from the pot into a serving bowl. Drain the pasta into a colander and then add pasta to the serving bowl and mix.

Serve the pasta onto the serving dishes, and ladle an appropriate amount of sauce on top of the pasta.

A wonderful enhancement to this sauce is to mix pecorino romano cheese and parmesan cheese and sprinkle on top of the sauce. This sauce can be refrigerated and/or frozen for later use.

# Sun-dried Tomatoes and Basil in Béchamel Sauce

## 2 Servings

5 sun-dried tomatoes

6-8 fresh basil leaves

½ pint heavy cream

½ lb. linguini pasta

1 small garlic clove

1 tablespoon butter (unsalted)

Fresh nutmeg

2 heaping tablespoons freshly grated fontina cheese

1 tablespoon Chicken Stock (see recipe)

1 heaping tablespoon grated parmesan cheese

1 egg yolk

1 tablespoon plus 1 teaspoon olive oil

Black pepper

Salt (sea)

In a large pot, add water to fill about ⅓ of the pot. Cook at medium-high heat. Bring the water to a boil and then add a heavy pinch of salt and 1 teaspoon of olive oil. Stir and bring the water to a boil again.

While the water for the pasta is coming to a boil, crush garlic clove. Remove the garlic skin, and place the garlic skin into a large sauté pan with 1 tablespoon of olive oil and butter. Cook at low heat for about 2 minutes until the oil gets hot. Once the oil and butter get hot, remove the garlic skin and discard.

When the water in the large pot comes to a boil for the second time, add the linguini by fanning it around the pot. After 1 minute, stir the pasta into the water so that the pasta doesn't stick. Cook the linguini for a total of 7 minutes.

Add the heavy cream to the sauté pan, 3 shakes of black pepper, and 5 grates of fresh nutmeg and whisk for 2 minutes and continue to cook at low heat. Thinly slice sun-dried tomatoes and take 6-8 fresh basil leaves and roll into a ball and slice same thinness as sun-dried tomatoes and set aside. Grate fontina cheese to fill a couple of heaping tablespoons. Add grated fontina cheese into cream mixture in the sauté pan, and mix with whisk until the cheese melts, about 3 minutes. Finely mince the garlic clove and set aside. Add the chicken stock, minced garlic, sun-dried tomatoes and basil to the sauté pan and mix with whisk. Reduce heat slightly and simmer for 1 minute and then stir with whisk several times by moving in a circular motion around the sauté pan until the sauce reduces (slightly thickens – syrupy).

When the pasta is done, pour about 2 tablespoons of cooking water from the pot into a serving bowl. Drain the pasta into a colander and then add pasta to the serving bowl and mix.

Once the mixture in the sauté pan reduces, add the pasta with grated parmesan cheese and mix. Then, add the egg yolk on top of the pasta and mix into pasta. Serve immediately.

# Chicken
## Chicken with Broccoli in White Wine Sauce

### 2 Servings

2 half-chicken breasts (boneless, skinless)

2 bunches broccoli

1 medium garlic clove

1 small yellow onion

½ lb. spaghetti

3 tablespoons grated parmesan cheese

All-purpose flour

1 cup Chicken Stock (see recipe)

1 splash dry white wine

2 tablespoons olive oil

3 tablespoons butter (unsalted)

Black pepper

Salt (sea)

Crush garlic clove; remove the garlic skin, and place the garlic skin into a large sauté pan with 2 tablespoons of olive oil and 1 tablespoon of butter. Cut off the top and bottom portions of the onion, and place them into the sauté pan with the onion side down and cook at low heat for about 2 minutes until the oil gets hot. Once the oil gets hot, remove the garlic skin and top and bottom portions of the onion and discard.

Add 5 shakes of black pepper (slightly less than ⅛ teaspoon) and a pinch of salt to the sauté pan. Cut and chop 2 slices of onion (about ¼ inch thick each slice) and add to sauté pan and cook at low heat for 4-5 minutes until the onions become transparent.

In a large pot, add water to fill about ⅓ of the pot. Cook at medium-high heat. Bring the water to a boil and then add a heavy pinch of salt and 1 teaspoon of olive oil. Stir and bring the water to a boil again.

Cut off the top portions (florets) of the broccoli and cut into smaller pieces. Fill a small sauce pan with 1 cup of chicken stock, and place the broccoli florets in the sauce pan and cook at low heat for 5 minutes.

Cut the half-chicken breasts twice lengthwise and then cut across about 6 times. In a separate dish, pour some all-purpose flour and mix with a pinch of black pepper and lightly flour each piece of chicken. Add the chicken pieces to the sauté pan, and cook at medium-low heat for about 7-8 minutes turning the chicken over once it gets color on one side. Finely mince the garlic clove and set aside. Once the chicken pieces have color on all sides, add 1 tablespoon of butter, minced garlic, and the broccoli with ⅓ cup of chicken stock and a splash of white wine and cook for an additional 8 minutes at medium-low heat.

Once the water in the large pot comes to a boil for a second time, add the spaghetti by fanning it around the pot. After one minute, stir the pasta into the water so that the pasta doesn't stick. Cook the spaghetti for a total of 6 minutes. When the pasta is done, pour about 2 tablespoons of cooking water from the pot into a serving bowl. Drain the pasta into a colander and then add pasta to serving bowl and mix.

When the chicken and broccoli mixture is done, pour it over the spaghetti and add 1 tablespoon of butter and parmesan cheese and mix and serve.

A creamy variation to this recipe is to mix in 2 tablespoons of Béchamel Sauce (see recipe) 2 minutes before the chicken with broccoli mixture is done.

# Chicken Risotto

## 4 Servings

2 half-chicken breasts (boneless, skinless)

1 ½ cups short grain rice

1 medium garlic clove

1 anchovy (flat fillet)

1 small yellow onion

1 small celery stalk

1 small whole carrot (peeled)

1 small summer squash

½ zucchini

Chicken Stock (see recipe) (a little more than 3 cups)

2 small pinches saffron

2 tablespoons olive oil

3 tablespoons grated parmesan cheese

2 tablespoons butter (unsalted)

Black pepper

Cut each half-chicken breast into about 14 pieces.  In a separate dish, pour some all-purpose flour and mix in a pinch of black pepper and lightly flour each piece of chicken and set aside.

Crush garlic clove; remove the garlic skin, and place the garlic skin into a large sauté pan with 2 tablespoons of olive oil.  Cut off the top and bottom portions of the onion, and place them into the sauté pan with the onion side down and cook at low heat for about 2 minutes until the oil gets hot. Once the oil gets hot, remove the garlic skin and the top and bottom portions of the onion and discard.

Chop and cut the celery stalk and whole carrot, and dice the onion into small pieces. Add the chopped vegetables into the sauté pan, and cook at low heat until the onions become transparent (about 4 minutes). Finely mince the garlic clove together with the anchovy fillet and add to the sauté pan and continue to cook at low heat for an additional minute.

In a separate sauce pan, add 3 cups of chicken stock, saffron, a pinch of black pepper, 1 tablespoon of butter, and bring to a boil at medium heat for about 2 minutes. Then add the rice, stir and cook at medium heat for 7 minutes; then reduce heat to low and cook for another 5 minutes.

Cut and quarter the summer squash and zucchini, but do not add the squash and zucchini to the sauté pan at this time. Add the floured chicken pieces to the sauté pan with the vegetables, and cook at medium-low heat, turning the chicken pieces, until all sides of all the pieces of chicken are cooked. Once the chicken pieces have color on all sides, which is about 15-20 minutes, add 1 tablespoon of butter. At this time, add the squash and the zucchini and mix with the chicken and other ingredients in the sauté pan. Cover the sauté pan with a lid that fits and continue to cook at medium-low heat for a maximum of 10 minutes.

Add 2 oz. of chicken stock to the rice in the sauce pan, and cook for an additional 3 minutes. Turn meat and vegetable mixture in the sauté pan up to medium heat, and add rice on top and let cook for 2 minutes. Then, mix the rice and reduce the heat on the sauté pan to low and cover and let simmer for a minimum of 10 minutes. Evenly sprinkle the parmesan cheese over the top of the rice. Let the cheese rest on the rice with no heat for about 30 seconds and serve.

# Chicken Cacciatore

## 2 Servings

4 chicken thighs

1 large can tomato sauce (29 oz.)

½ lb. spaghetti

1 small garlic clove

1 anchovy (flat fillet)

1 small yellow onion

1 celery stalk

1 whole carrot (peeled)

1 splash dry white wine

3-4 fresh basil leaves

1 sprig fresh tarragon

All-purpose flour

6 oz. Chicken Stock (see recipe)

2 tablespoons plus 1 teaspoon olive oil

1 tablespoon grated parmesan cheese

1 tablespoon grated asiago cheese

Black pepper (pinch)

Salt (sea)

Take the chicken thighs and cut the top of the bone so that the marrow will bleed. In a separate deep dish, pour some all-purpose flour and mix in ⅛ teaspoon of black pepper. Lightly flour each chicken thigh and set aside.

Crush garlic clove; remove the garlic skin, and place the garlic skin into a large sauté pan with 2 tablespoons of olive oil. Cut off the top and bottom portions of the onion, and place them into the sauté pan with the onion side down and cook at low heat for about 2 minutes until the oil gets hot. Once the oil gets hot, remove the garlic skin and the top and bottom portions of the onion and discard.

Add the chicken thighs to the sauté pan with skin side down and cook for 15 minutes (7-8 minutes on each side), turning to get color on both sides. While this is cooking, cut and dice the onion and quarter and dice the whole carrot and celery stalk. Add celery, carrots, and onions to the sauté pan and cook at low heat for about 4 minutes. Once you have color on both sides of the chicken, add a splash of dry white wine with a pinch of salt and a pinch black pepper on top of the chicken. Finely mince the garlic clove together with the anchovy fillet and add to the sauté pan and cook at low heat for about 1 minute. Chop the tarragon and basil and add them to the sauté pan. Cook at low heat for an additional 5-6 minutes, turning the ingredients in the sauté pan occasionally.

Add the tomato sauce into the sauté pan. Pour the chicken stock into the empty tomato sauce can. Swirl the chicken stock around the empty can to collect any tomato sauce residue; then, pour the chicken stock together with the residue into the sauté pan. Cover the sauté pan and cook at low heat for 45 minutes.

About 20-25 minutes before the sauce is done, begin the pasta. In a large pot, add water to fill about ⅓ of the pot. Cook at medium-high heat. Bring the water to a boil and then add a heavy pinch of salt and 1 teaspoon of olive oil. Stir and bring the water to a boil again. At this point, add the spaghetti by fanning it around the pot. After one minute, stir the pasta into the water so that the pasta doesn't stick. Cook the spaghetti for a total of 6 minutes. When the pasta is done, pour about 2 tablespoons of cooking water from the pot into the serving bowl. Drain the pasta into a colander and then add pasta to serving bowl and mix.

Serve the pasta and an appropriate amount of sauce and place 2 chicken thighs on top of each serving. Sprinkle parmesan and asiago cheese and serve.

In addition to the ingredients in this recipe, I also like to add about 2-3 oz. of sliced button mushrooms or ½ dozen split olives or 4 artichoke hearts. These additional ingredients can be added 15 minutes before the sauce is done.

# Chicken Cacciatore II

## 3 Servings

6 chicken thighs

1 ½ large cans tomato sauce (29 oz.)

1 slice of pancetta (¼ inch thick)

½ lb. spaghetti

1 small garlic clove

1 ½ anchovy (flat fillet)

1 small yellow onion

1 celery stalk

1 whole carrot (peeled)

1 splash dry white wine

3-4 fresh basil leaves

Fresh tarragon

Fresh nutmeg

All-purpose flour

6 oz. Chicken Stock (see recipe)

2 tablespoons plus 1 teaspoon olive oil

1 tablespoon butter (unsalted)

1 tablespoon freshly grated pecorino romano cheese

1 tablespoon grated parmesan cheese

Black pepper

Salt (sea)

Take the chicken thighs and cut the top of the bone so that the marrow will bleed. In a separate deep dish, pour some all-purpose flour and mix in ⅛ teaspoon of black pepper. Lightly flour each chicken thigh and set aside.

Crush garlic clove; remove the garlic skin, and place the garlic skin into a large sauté pan with 2 tablespoons of olive oil. Cut off the top and bottom portions of the onion, and place them into the sauté pan with the onion side down and cook at low heat for about 2 minutes until the oil gets hot. Once the oil gets hot, remove the garlic skin and the top and bottom portions of the onion and discard.

Take the slice of pancetta and dice into about 16 pieces and add to sauté pan and cook at low heat for 2-3 minutes until the pancetta gets color. Add 5 shakes of black pepper (slightly less than ⅛ teaspoon) and 5 grates of fresh nutmeg into the sauté pan. Add the chicken thighs to the sauté pan with skin side down and cook for 15 minutes (7-8 minutes on each side), turning to get color on both sides.

While the chicken thighs are cooking, cut and dice the small onion, and quarter and dice the whole carrot and celery stalk. Add celery, carrots, and onions to the sauté pan and cook at low heat for about 4 minutes. Once there is color on both sides of the chicken, add the butter and a splash of white wine to the sauté pan. Finely mince the garlic clove together with the anchovy fillet and add to the sauté pan and cook at low heat for about 1 minute. Chop the tarragon and the basil and add them to the sauté pan. Cook at low heat for an additional 5-6 minutes, turning the ingredients in the sauté pan occasionally.

Add the tomato sauce into the sauté pan. Pour the chicken stock into the empty tomato sauce can. Swirl the chicken stock around the empty can to collect any tomato sauce residue; then, pour the chicken stock together with the residue into the sauté pan. Cover the sauté pan and cook at low heat for 45 minutes.

About 20-25 minutes before the sauce is done, begin the pasta. In a large pot, add water to fill about ⅓ of the pot. Cook at medium-high heat. Bring the water to a boil; then, add a heavy pinch of salt and 1 teaspoon of olive oil. Stir and bring the water to a boil again. At this point, add the spaghetti by fanning it around the pot. After one minute, stir the pasta into the water so that the pasta doesn't stick. Cook the spaghetti for a total of 6 minutes. When the pasta is done, pour about 2 tablespoons of cooking water from the pot into the serving bowl. Drain the pasta into a colander and then add pasta to serving bowl and mix.

Serve the pasta and an appropriate amount of sauce and place 2 chicken thighs on top of each serving. Sprinkle parmesan and pecorino romano chesse and serve.

# Chicken Saltimbocca

## 2 Servings

1 half-chicken breast (boneless, skinless)

2 slices prosciutto di Parma

1 small garlic clove

6 fresh sage leaves

2 splashes dry white wine

All-purpose flour

1 tablespoon olive oil

5 tablespoons Chicken Stock (see recipe)

2 tablespoons plus 1 teaspoon butter (unsalted)

Black pepper

 

Clean the half-chicken breast by trimming off any excess fat, rinsing each piece in cool water, and patting each piece dry with a clean, white paper towel. Cut each half-chicken breast horizontally (parallel to the cutting surface) beginning at the thicker end and making two fillets. Then, lightly pound each fillet and set them aside. Tear the stem off of 2 fresh sage leaves and then tear each leaf in half. Evenly place two pieces of sage leaf on top of each chicken fillet. Take a pinch of black pepper and rub it into the top of each piece of sage leaf and onto the top of the fillet. Place a slice of prosciutto di Parma on top of each chicken fillet, sage, and black pepper. In a separate dish, pour some all-purpose flour and mix in ⅛ teaspoon of black pepper. Lightly flour each chicken fillet with leaf and prosciutto and set aside.

Crush garlic clove; remove the garlic skin, and place the garlic skin into a large sauté pan with the olive oil and 1 tablespoon of butter and cook at low heat for about 2 minutes until the oil and butter get hot. Once the oil gets hot, remove the garlic skin and discard. Finely mince the garlic clove and set aside.

Tear the stems off of 4 fresh sage leaves and tear them in half and add them to the oil/butter mixture in the sauté pan together with a pinch of black pepper and the minced garlic and cook for 3 minutes at low heat. Add the chicken fillets to the sauté pan with the prosciutto side down. Cook the chicken fillets for 3 ½ minutes at medium-low heat. Add 3 tablespoons of chicken stock (depending on how much liquid there is in the sauté pan). At this time, add a splash of dry white wine and 1 tablespoon of butter. Turn chicken fillets over and cook for an additional 3 ½ minutes.

Preheat oven to bake at 350 degrees. Remove the chicken fillets and place them in a baking dish (large enough to fit the chicken fillets) with the prosciutto side up. Whisk the ingredients* in the sauté pan at low heat until the mixture starts to reduce; then pour over the chicken fillets. Put the baking dish into the oven at 350 degrees for 5 minutes and then serve.

*If more liquid is needed, add 1 oz. of chicken stock, ¼ oz. of dry white wine and 1 teaspoon of butter.

# Chicken with Marsala Sauce

## 3 Servings

3 half-chicken breasts (boneless, skinless)

8 oz. mushrooms

3 tablespoons marsala wine

1 small garlic clove

1 oz. Chicken Stock (see recipe)

Fresh nutmeg

4 tablespoons butter (unsalted)

All-purpose flour

1 tablespoon olive oil

Black pepper

Clean the mushrooms by rinsing them in cold water and cut them into slices and set aside. In a separate dish, pour some all-purpose flour and mix in ⅛ teaspoon of black pepper. Clean the half-chicken breasts by trimming off any excess fat, rinse each piece in cool water and pat each piece dry with a clean, white paper towel. Cut each half-chicken breast horizontally (parallel to the cutting surface) beginning at the thicker end and making two fillets. Then, lightly pound and lightly flour each fillet and set them aside.

Crush garlic clove; remove the garlic skin, and place the garlic skin into a large sauté pan with 1 tablespoon of olive oil and 1 tablespoon of butter and cook at low heat for about 2 minutes until the oil gets hot. Once the oil and butter get hot, remove the garlic skin and discard.

Add 5 grates of fresh nutmeg, 3 shakes of black pepper, and sliced mushroom, and cook at low heat for about 4-5 minutes. After a few minutes, turn the mushrooms and continue cooking. At this point, add 2 tablespoons of marsala wine. Finely mince the garlic clove and add to the sauté pan. Cook for an additional 1 minute at medium heat; then remove the mushrooms from the sauté pan and set aside.

Shake off any excess flour from the chicken fillets and add 3 pieces to the sauté pan together with 1 tablespoon of butter. Cook for 3 minutes on each side on low heat (only a few pieces at a time fit in the sauté pan). Remove the chicken fillets from the pan; then cook the other 3 pieces adding an additional 1 tablespoon of butter and cook in the same manner as before. Then remove the fillets and set all of the fillets aside.

Add the mushrooms back into the sauté pan together with chicken stock, 1 tablespoon of butter, and 1 tablespoon of marsala wine and cook at medium-low heat for 2 minutes until the sauce slightly thickens. Add the chicken pieces to the sauté pan with the mushrooms; mix and cook for another 2 minutes and serve by placing the chicken pieces on a plate and pouring the mushroom mixture on top.

If you prefer a creamy variation to this recipe, 2 tablespoons of Béchamel Sauce (see recipe) may be added at the end when the chicken pieces and the mushrooms are added back into the sauté pan and cooked for another 2 minutes. Another variation to this recipe is to make it without mushrooms.

# Chicken Primavera

## 4 Servings

2 half-chicken breasts (boneless, skinless)

2 slices of prosciutto de Parma

1 medium tomato

1 small garlic clove

2 fresh sage leaves

½ sprig fresh rosemary

5 leaves fresh oregano

1 tablespoon balsamic vinegar

5 tablespoons butter (unsalted)

2 tablespoons of Chicken Stock (see recipe)

Fontina cheese

All-purpose flour

4 tablespoons olive oil

Black pepper (pinch)

Salt (sea) (pinch)

Clean the half-chicken breasts by trimming off any excess fat, rinse each piece in cool water, and pat each piece dry with a clean, white paper towel. Cut each half-chicken breast horizontally (parallel to the cutting surface) beginning at the thicker end and making two fillets. Then, lightly pound each fillet and set them aside. In a separate dish, pour some all-purpose flour and mix in ⅛ teaspoon of black pepper. Lightly flour each chicken fillet and set them aside.

In a separate deep dish, marinate four slices of the tomato in 2 tablespoons of olive oil, chopped oregano, balsamic vinegar, with a pinch of black pepper, and a pinch of salt and set aside.

Crush garlic clove; remove the garlic skin, and place the garlic skin into a large sauté pan with 2 tablespoons of olive oil. Cook at low heat for about 2 minutes until the oil gets hot. Once the oil gets hot, remove the garlic skin and discard.

Finely mince garlic and chop the sage leaves and add to the sauté pan. Continue to keep the heat on the sauté pan at low. Remove the rosemary leaves from their stem, chop the rosemary leaves, and add them to the sauté pan. Cook for 2 minutes at low heat; then add the floured chicken fillets and cook for 2-4 minutes.

Cut each slice of prosciutto in half. Turn the chicken over after 2 minutes and add 1 tablespoon of butter into the sauté pan and place a slice of prosciutto on top of each piece of chicken fillet. Add the chicken stock to the mixture in the sauté pan and bring to a boil, about 2 minutes; then, place a marinated tomato slice on top of the prosciutto on each piece of chicken fillet. Cut four slices of fontina cheese. Cut each slice large enough so that the cheese overlaps the sliced tomato; then, place a slice of fontina cheese on top of each piece of tomato. Continue to cook at low heat for 3 minutes; then remove each piece of chicken fillet and place them in a baking dish (large enough to fit four chicken fillets).

Preheat oven to bake at 375 degrees. Add an additional tablespoon of butter to the sauté pan, and bring it to a boil while whisking until the butter is melted, mixed, and reduced. Pour over the chicken with prosciutto, tomato, and cheese. Place the baking dish in the oven, and bake for 10 minutes or until the cheese is melted. Serve immediately.

# Chicken Parmigiano

## 2 Servings

1 half-chicken breast (boneless, skinless)

Plain or Italian bread crumbs or
Ritz crackers (one roll of crackers finely crumbled)

All-purpose flour

¼ pint of heavy cream

1 ½ cups Marinara Sauce (see recipe)

1 medium garlic clove

1 anchovy (flat fillet)

1 egg yolk

½ cup shredded mozzarella cheese (whole milk)
(acceptable to use packaged shredded mozzarella cheese)

2 tablespoons olive oil

2 tablespoons parmesan cheese

Black pepper

Clean the half-chicken breasts by trimming off any excess fat, rinsing each piece in cool water, and then pat each piece dry with a clean, white paper towel. Slice each half-chicken breast horizontally (parallel to the cutting surface) beginning at the thicker end and making two fillets. Then, lightly pound each fillet and set them aside.

In a separate dish, pour some all-purpose flour and add ⅛ teaspoon of black pepper and mix into the flour. In a separate bowl or deep dish (wide enough to fit chicken fillet), place one egg yolk with ¼ pint of heavy cream and whisk together. In a third dish, pour some bread crumbs (or cracker crumbs) together with 1 tablespoon of parmesan cheese and mix.

The first step is to lightly flour the chicken fillets entirely (on both sides); the second step is to take the chicken fillets and immerse each one into the egg and cream wash and cover them completely; and the third step is to cover each chicken fillet with the bread crumbs/parmesan cheese mixture (or cracker crumbs/parmesan cheese mixture), and lightly pat the crumbs onto each fillet and set aside.

Crush garlic clove; remove the garlic skin, and place the garlic skin into a large sauté pan with olive oil and cook at low heat for about 2 minutes until the oil gets hot. Once the oil is hot, remove the garlic skin and discard. Finely mince the garlic clove together with anchovy fillet and add the mixture to the sauté pan and cook at low heat for 2 minutes.

Place the two breaded chicken fillets into the sauté pan and cook at low heat. Once one side of the breaded chicken fillet becomes golden brown in color, about 3 minutes, turn it over and cook the other side until it becomes golden brown in color, about another 3 minutes.

While the chicken fillets are cooking, preheat oven to bake at 400 degrees. Line the bottom of a baking dish (a baking dish large enough to fit two chicken fillets) with about ¼ cup of Marinara Sauce. Once the chicken fillets are cooked, place them on top of the Marinara Sauce in the baking dish. Take one heaping tablespoon of parmesan cheese and evenly sprinkle the cheese on top of each breaded chicken fillet. Add an equal amount of shredded mozzarella cheese to the top of each breaded chicken fillet. Then, add the rest of the Marinara Sauce, about 1 ¼ cups, to the top and around each fillet and bake in the oven for 25 minutes.

The bread/cracker crumb combination for the exterior of the chicken fillet can either be all bread crumbs or all cracker crumbs or a combination of both. I prefer a 50/50 combination of bread crumbs and cracker crumbs. My wife prefers only bread crumbs. A variation to this recipe is to make the breaded chicken fillets without the Marinara Sauce and without the mozzarella cheese on top. Instead, place a small anchovy on top of each breaded chicken fillet after sprinkling the parmesan cheese, and then squeeze the juice of ¼ lemon and then bake in the oven at 400 degrees for 10-15 minutes.

# Steak

## Tenderloin Steaks

### 4 Servings

4 tenderloin steaks (about 6 oz. each)

1 medium garlic clove

1 sprig fresh rosemary

1 tablespoon balsamic vinegar

2 tablespoons beef broth (low-sodium)

1 splash dry red wine

All-purpose flour

2 tablespoons butter (unsalted)

3 tablespoons plus ½ teaspoon olive oil

Black pepper

Salt (sea)


Completely clean each tenderloin steak of any suet (solid white fat). Mince garlic clove and set aside. Remove the rosemary leaves from their stem, chop the rosemary leaves, and set aside.

In a deep dish, add 3 tablespoons of olive oil, minced garlic, chopped rosemary, balsamic vinegar, beef broth, red wine, ¼ teaspoon of salt, ¼ teaspoon of black pepper and mix. Add the tenderloin steaks to the dish. Marinate the tenderloin steaks in the refrigerator for 12-24 hours, turning over the steaks about half-way through the marinating process so that all portions of the steaks get marinated.

When you are ready to cook the tenderloin steaks, take a separate dish, pour some all-purpose flour and mix in a pinch of black pepper. Take each tenderloin steak and pat it dry with a clean, white paper towel and lightly flour.

In a small sauté pan, add ½ tablespoon of olive oil with 1 tablespoon of butter and cook at medium-low heat. Bring to a boil and as the butter starts to brown, add the tenderloin steaks and cook for 3 minutes on each side at medium heat. After the tenderloin steaks are cooked, remove the steaks from the sauté pan and place them onto the serving plate. Add to the sauté pan 4 tablespoons of marinade and 1 tablespoon of butter and whisk at medium heat. Reduce the sauce until it slightly thickens. Pour the sauce over the tenderloin steaks and serve immediately.

Before cooking the tenderloin steaks, wrap 1-2 slice(s) of pancetta or 1 slice of proscuitto di Parma around each steak and sprinkle a grate of nutmeg over each steak. You will be amazed how this enhances the taste of the steaks. When I make the Tenderloin Steaks, I start out by making my Marinated Steak House Tomatoes (see recipe). With the Tenderloin Steaks, I serve my Roasted Potatoes Rosemary and Green Beans (see recipes). I find this to be a wonderful combination.

# Journados Favrita

## (Stuffed Tenderloin)

### 2 Servings

2 prime tenderloin steaks (about 5 ½ oz. each)

2-4 slices of prosciutto di Parma

2 oz. brie cheese

1 small garlic clove

1 tablespoon butter (unsalted)

All purpose flour

Fresh nutmeg

1 tablespoon Chicken Stock (see recipe)

Splash marsala wine

Black pepper


Completely clean each tenderloin steak of and any suet (solid white fat). Shape and pat each tenderloin steak so that they are easier to butterfly. Butterfly each tenderloin steak and place a slice or two of prosciutto to cover the inside of each butterflied steak. Take about 1 oz. of brie cheese and place it in the center of the prosciutto of each steak and close. In a separate deep dish, pour some all-purpose flour and mix in a pinch of black pepper. Lightly flour the exterior of each steak covering all sides.

In a small sauté pan, add 3 small pieces of garlic with the butter and melt at low heat until the butter begins to brown. Increase the heat to medium-low and place the floured tenderloin steaks in the sauté pan. Add 3 grates of fresh nutmeg with 1 shake of black pepper on each steak and cook for 3 minutes on each side.

Remove the steaks from the pan and place onto the serving plate. Add 1 tablespoon of chicken stock and a splash of marsala wine to the sauté pan. Whisk the ingredients at medium-low heat for about 2-3 minutes until they become blended with the scrapings to form a gravy. Pour the gravy over the steaks and serve immediately.

I recommend serving the Tournados Favrita with my Marinated Steak House Tomatoes and my Marinated Asparagus or my Garlic and Spinach (see recipes).

# Seafood
## Shrimp and Scallops in Pesto Sauce

**2 Servings**

8 jumbo cooked shrimp (size: 15/20 lb. count)

8 large scallops

½ lb. linguini

1 ½ medium garlic clove

2 tablespoons plus 1 teaspoon olive oil

1 tablespoon butter (unsalted)

3 tablespoons Pesto Sauce (see recipe)

2-3 tablespoons parmesan cheese (depending on taste)

Salt (sea) (heavy pinch)


In a large pot, add water to fill about ⅓ of the pot. Cook at medium-high heat. Bring the water to a boil and then add a heavy pinch of salt and 1 teaspoon of olive oil. Stir and bring the water to a boil again.

While the water for the pasta is coming to a boil, crush the garlic cloves. Remove the garlic skins, and place the garlic skins into a large sauté pan with 2 tablespoons of olive oil and cook at low heat for about 2 minutes until the oil gets hot. Once the oil gets hot, remove the garlic skin and discard.

When the water in the large pot comes to a boil for the second time, add the linguini by fanning it around the pot. After one minute, stir the pasta into the water so that the pasta doesn't stick. Cook the linguini for a total of 7 minutes.

Finely mince the garlic cloves and add to the sauté pan. Remove the tails from the shrimp and make sure that they are cleaned and deveined. Add the shrimp to the sauté pan and cook the shrimp on each side for 1 minute. Remove the shrimp from the sauté pan and set aside. Place scallops in the sauté pan and cook until they turn color, about 2 ½ minutes on each side. Remove the scallops and, also, remove the garlic and turn off the heat on the pan.

Add the butter and allow the butter to melt by using the heat from the pan (without adding heat). Spread 1 ½ tablespoons of pesto sauce in the sauté pan and resume cooking at low heat. Lay shrimp and scallops separately on top of the pesto sauce. Bring to a boil and stir the shrimp and scallops so that they are covered with the pesto sauce.

When the pasta is done, pour about 2 tablespoons of cooking water from the pot into the serving bowl. Drain the pasta into a colander and then add pasta to serving bowl and mix.

Add pasta to the sauté pan with shrimp and scallops and pesto and then mix. Add the rest of the pesto sauce (1 ½ tablespoons) on top of the pasta and carefully mix. After mixing thoroughly, turn off heat and add a small amount of parmesan cheese on top and serve immediately.

# Shrimp and Scallops "Alfredo"

## 2 Servings

4 jumbo cooked shrimp (size: 15/20 lb. count)

4 large scallops

½ lb. linguini pasta

1 medium garlic clove

1 heaping tablespoon freshly grated fontina cheese

¼ pint heavy cream

1 egg yolk

Fresh nutmeg

1 tablespoon butter (unsalted)

1 tablespoon plus 1 teaspoon olive oil

Parmesan cheese

Black pepper

Salt (sea)


In a large pot, add water to fill about ⅓ of the pot. Cook at medium-high heat. Bring the water to a boil and then add a heavy pinch of salt and 1 teaspoon of olive oil. Stir and bring the water to a boil again.

While the water for the pasta is coming to a boil, crush garlic clove. Remove the garlic skin, and place the garlic skin into a large sauté pan with 1 tablespoon of olive oil and cook at low heat for about 2 minutes until the oil gets hot. Once the oil is hot, remove the garlic skin and discard. Mince the garlic clove and set aside.

When the water in the large pot comes to a boil for the second time, add linguini by fanning it around the pot. After 1 minute, stir pasta into water so that the pasta doesn't stick. Cook the linguini for a total of 7 minutes.

While the pasta is cooking, add 2 pinches of black pepper, minced garlic, 4-5 grates of fresh nutmeg, and 1 tablespoon of butter to the sauté pan.

Take the cooked shrimp and remove the tails and make sure that they are clean and deveined. Add shrimp and scallops to the sauté pan and cook at medium-low heat for 3 minutes on each side.

Reduce the heat of the sauté pan to low heat and whisk in the heavy cream. Add a pinch of black pepper and 3 grates of nutmeg. Whisk the ingredients in the sauté pan for about 2 minutes. Add grated Fontina cheese into the cream mixture in the sauté pan and whisk until the cheese melts, about 3 minutes.

When the pasta is done, pour about 2 tablespoons of cooking water from the pot into a serving bowl. Drain pasta in colander and then add pasta to serving bowl and mix.

Then, add the pasta to the sauté pan with shrimp and scallops and mix. Add one egg yolk and mix well. Add a heaping tablespoon of parmesan cheese, mix, and serve immediately.

# Personal Notes

# Fish with Pesto Sauce

## 2 Servings

¾ lb. scrod or

¾ lb. swordfish

Pesto Sauce (see recipe)

Black pepper

## Scrod:

Preheat oven to bake at 400 degrees. Place about ¾ lb. of scrod in a baking dish. Lightly sprinkle on top with black pepper. Add a generous amount of pesto sauce to the top of the scrod.

Place the baking dish in the oven, and cook for 25-30 minutes (depending on the heat of your oven).

## Swordfish:

Preheat oven to bake at 400 degrees. Place about ¾ lb. of swordfish in a baking dish. Lightly sprinkle on top with black pepper. Add a generous amount of pesto sauce to the top of the swordfish.

Place the baking dish in the oven, and cook for 35-40 minutes (depending on the heat of your oven).

A variation of this recipe is to bake the fish with ½ cup of Marinara Sauce (see recipe). I recommend that you serve these fish dishes with my Aglio Burro Pasta (see recipe). The scrod or swordfish with pesto sauce has a very intense flavor; therefore, it would be best to complement the dish with my Aglio Burro Pasta, which is mild in flavor.

# Shrimp Piccante con Risotto

## 2 Servings

8 jumbo cooked shrimp (size: 15/20 lb. count)

1 cup rice (short grain)

1 small garlic clove

1 small yellow onion

1 celery stalk

1 whole carrot (peeled)

1 small summer squash

1 anchovy (flat fillet)

2 cups Chicken Stock (see recipe)

All-purpose flour

½ fresh lemon

Dijon mustard (2 heaping tablespoons)

Mayonnaise (2 heaping tablespoons)

Crushed red pepper (generous pinch)

Grated parmesan cheese (2 heaping tablespoons)

2 tablespoons butter (unsalted)

2 tablespoons olive oil

Saffron (generous pinch)

Fresh nutmeg

Black pepper

Crush garlic clove; remove the garlic skin, and place the garlic skin into a large sauté pan with the olive oil. Cut off the top and bottom portions of the onion and place them into the sauté pan with the onion side down and cook at low heat for about 2 minutes until the oil gets hot. Once the oil gets hot, remove the garlic skin and top and bottom portions of the onion and discard.

Cut and chop the onion, celery stalk, and whole carrot and place them in the sauté pan with 2 pinches of black pepper, 5-6 grates of fresh nutmeg, and 1 tablespoon of butter. Cook these ingredients in the sauté pan at low heat until the onion becomes transparent, about 6 minutes. Finely mince the garlic clove together with the anchovy fillet and add to the sauté pan and continue to cook at low heat for an additional minute.

Slice the summer squash by cutting it lengthwise; then slicing it into pieces and set the pieces aside.

In a separate sauce pan, add chicken stock, a generous pinch of saffron, and one tablespoon of butter and cook at medium-low heat. When the chicken stock begins to boil, about 2-3 minutes, add rice. Stir the rice and cook for 10 minutes stirring every few minutes.

While the rice is cooking, add the summer squash to the sauté pan. After the summer squash has been in the sauté pan for 3 minutes, remove the celery, carrots, onion, and squash and set all of these ingredients aside in a separate dish.

Take the cooked shrimp and remove the tails and make sure that they are cleaned and deveined. In a separate dish, pour some all-purpose flour and mix in ⅛ teaspoon of black pepper. Lightly flour the shrimp and set aside. In another dish, place the juice of ½ lemon, mayonnaise, dijon mustard, and a generous pinch of crushed red pepper and mix well. Dip the shrimp into the mayonnaise/mustard mixture and make sure that they are thoroughly covered. Add the shrimp to the sauté pan and cook for 3 minutes on each side at medium heat. Once the shrimp are cooked, remove them from the sauté pan and place them in a separate dish.

Pour out ½ of the oil from the sauté pan and discard. Then, add the celery, carrots, onions, and summer squash back into the sauté pan. Add all of the rice mixture (including any liquid) to the sauté pan and mix the rice with the vegetables and cook for an additional 5 minutes at medium-low heat. After 5 minutes, sprinkle 3 heaping tablespoons of parmesan cheese all over the top of the rice and vegetables. Serve equally onto two serving plates. Once served, add the shrimp to the top of the rice.

# Scrod Siciliano

## 2 Servings

¾ lb. scrod

1 large can of whole tomatoes (about 29 oz.)

1 celery stalk

1 whole carrot (peeled)

1 small yellow onion

8-10 pitted olives

1 small garlic clove

1 anchovy (flat fillet)

1 sprig fresh tarragon

1 tablespoon Pesto Sauce (see recipe)

½ lb. spaghetti

2 tablespoons Chicken Stock (see recipe)

1 tablespoon butter (unsalted)

2 tablespoons plus 1 teaspoon olive oil

Black pepper

Salt (sea)

Remove the whole tomatoes from the can and slice each tomato into small pieces and set aside with any juice from the can. Cut and dice celery stalk, whole carrot, and onion and set aside (do not discard the top and bottom portions of the onion). Split the pitted olives and set aside.

77

Crush garlic clove; remove the garlic skin, and place the garlic skin into a large sauté pan with 2 tablespoons of olive oil and the butter together with the top and bottom portions of the onion, with the onion side down, and cook at low heat for about 2 minutes until the oil gets hot. Once the oil gets hot, remove the garlic skin and the top and bottom portions of the onion and discard

Add the celery, carrots, onions, and a generous pinch of black pepper to the sauté pan and cook at medium-low heat for about 5 minutes mixing and turning occasionally until the onions become transparent. Finely mince the garlic clove together with anchovy fillet and add to the sauté pan. Remove the tarragon leaves from their stem, chop the tarragon leaves, and add them to the sauté pan and continue to cook at low heat for an additional minute. At this point, add the pesto sauce, chopped olives, chicken stock and sliced tomatoes, with any juice, and continue to cook at medium-low heat for ½ hour. After ½ hour add the scrod to sauce in the sauté pan, sprinkle a pinch of black pepper on top of the scrod then ladle some sauce on top of the fish. Cover and cook for 25-30 minutes at same medium-low heat. For the last 5 minutes, decrease the heat to low heat and move the scrod in the pan and add more sauce on top of scrod.

While the fish and the sauce are cooking, begin to make the pasta. In a large pot add water to reach about ⅓ of the pot. Cook at medium-high heat. Bring to a boil and then add a heavy pinch of salt and 1 teaspoon of olive oil. Stir and bring the water to a boil again. At this point, add ½ lb. of spaghetti by fanning it around the pot. After one minute, stir the pasta into the water so that the pasta doesn't stick. Cook the spaghetti for a total of 6 minutes. Pour about 2 tablespoons of cooking water from the pot into a serving bowl. Drain the pasta into a colander and then add pasta to serving bowl and mix.

Remove the scrod from the sauté pan; add the sauce from the sauté pan to the pasta and mix. Serve the pasta and an appropriate amount of sauce and place the scrod on top of each serving.

This recipe can also be made with the regular tomato sauce by replacing the large can of whole tomatoes with a large can of tomato sauce. My preference is to make this recipe with whole tomatoes.

# Sole/Flounder Au Gratin

## 2 Servings

4 fillets of sole/flounder (acceptable to use either fish) (about ¾ lb. total)

2 tablespoons plain bread crumbs or Ritz crackers (finely crumbled)

1 sprig fresh tarragon leaves

1 tablespoon dry white wine

1 small garlic clove

1/3 fresh lemon

1 ½ tablespoon grated parmesan cheese

2 tablespoons olive oil

4 teaspoons butter (unsalted)

Black pepper

Salt (sea)

Finely mince garlic and set aside. Remove the tarragon leaves from their stem, chop the tarragon leaves, and set them aside.

Place the sole/flounder fillets into a baking dish with the olive oil, dry white wine, minced garlic, chopped tarragon, 2 generous pinches of black pepper and a pinch of salt. Marinate the sole/flounder for one hour, turning over the fillets at least once during that period of time.

Once the fillets have marinated for one hour, squeeze and add the lemon juice, evenly sprinkle the grated parmesan cheese, and evenly sprinkle at least 2 tablespoons of plain bread crumbs or cracker crumbs over all of the 4 fillets.

Preheat oven to bake at 400 degrees.  Place 1 teaspoon of butter on top of each fillet and cook the fillets in the oven at 400 degrees for 25-30 minutes. The color of the bread crumbs or cracker crumbs should be golden brown.

I recommend serving this dish with Aglio Burro Pasta with thin spaghetti and Sautéed Vegetables: Summer Squash and Plum Tomatoes  (see recipes).  The tastes definitely complement each other. The vegetables also add both flavor and color.

# Grocery List

These ingredients are frequently used in my recipes. I strongly recommend that you have these ingredients in your kitchen at all times.

### CONDIMENTS
All-Purpose Flour
Balsamic Vinegar
Beef Broth (low sodium)
Black Pepper (grounded) (peppercorn)
Bread Crumbs
Croutons
Dijon Mustard
Mayonnaise
Red Pepper (crushed)
Red Wine Vinegar
Ritz Crackers
Olive Oil
Pine Nuts
Salt (sea)
Worcestershire Sauce

### CANNED FISH
Anchovies (flat fillets)
Tuna Fish (solid white albacore)

### DAIRY
Asiago Cheese
Brie Cheese
Butter (unsalted)
Cheddar Cheese
Eggs
Fontina Cheese
Heavy Cream
Mozzarella Cheese (whole milk)
    (ball and shredded)
Parmesan Cheese (grated)
Romano Cheese (grated)

## FRUITS
Lemons

## FRESH HERBS
Basil
Nutmeg
Oregano
Rosemary
Parsley
Saffron
Sage
Tarragon

## PASTA

Elbow Macaroni
Fettuccine
Lasagna Noodles
Linguini
Rigatoni
Spaghetti (regular and thin)
Ziti

## VEGETABLES
Black Olives (pitted)
Carrots
Celery
Cannellini Beans (can)
Garlic
Onion
Red Kidney Beans (can)
Red Potatoes
Rice (short grain)
Spinach (frozen)
Tomato Sauce (can)
Whole Tomatoes (can)

## WINE
Red Wine (dry – Chianti)
Sweet Wine (Marsala)
White Wine (dry – Orvietto)

# Michael's Glossary and Notes

**Black Pepper** – I often use grounded black pepper, and I like to describe my uses by shakes. In my recipes, I "shake" the ground pepper from the small holes on top of grounded black pepper container. Five shakes of ground pepper are slightly less than ⅛ of a teaspoon. I have, however, used a grinder with black peppercorns. This is also acceptable, but be aware that the ground peppercorn comes out very coarse.

**Bottled Water** – Whenever possible, I strongly recommend that you cook pasta with bottled water. Tap water is usually influenced by local water systems as well as the environment, which can alter adversely the taste of the sauce that you are using. Bottled water is chemical free; therefore, you have more control over the outcome of your recipe.

**Butter** – I always use unsalted butter. By using unsalted butter, you are able to control the quantity of salt in a recipe.

**Chicken Stock** – Chicken stock is the basis of all chicken, some beef, and some fish dishes and even some sauces. Whenever you are reading one of my recipes, and I refer to chicken stock as one of the ingredients, I strongly suggest that you use fresh chicken stock. Fresh homemade chicken stock will enhance the flavor of dishes and can be used to deglaze with wine and butter for gravy.

**Half-Chicken Breast (boneless, skinless)** – Most of my recipes call for "½ chicken breast." I would like to clarify this by saying that when you buy a package of chicken breasts from the store, one portion is one-half of the chicken breast. That one portion is what I call "½ chicken breast."

**Chicken Cleansing** – I strongly suggest that you clean chicken by rinsing it with cold water; then, pat dry with a clean, white paper towel and trim off any excess fat. Be sure to always wash your hands thoroughly after handling chicken.

**Butterflying a Half-Chicken Breast** – Take a very sharp knife (preferably a French knife) in your dominant hand. Place your other hand on top of the half-chicken breast with your palm touching the top of the piece of breast. Slice into the thick portion of the chicken breast, then cut the breast horizontally (parallel to the cutting surface). Do not cut about ¼ inch of the thick portion of the breast. Be very careful and slice the half-chicken breast very slowly, taking extra care when you slice through the thinner portion.

**Filleting a Half-Chicken Breast** – Follow the same steps as you would to butterfly a half-chicken breast, except slice the chicken breast completely without leaving any portion uncut.

**Cracker Crumbs** – I do use Ritz cracker crumbs in a couple of my recipes. They must be finely crushed and ground when using them instead of bread crumbs. I crush the crackers with my hands while the crackers are still wrapped. If the crackers are not finely crushed, then I use the back of a large spoon to crush them.

**Deglazing** – This is a process that I use when I want to scrape food particles from a roasting pan. I take a small amount of liquid, usually chicken stock or wine, and I put it into the roasting pan while heating the pan at medium-low heat. Use a whisk to scrape the pan of food particles. This is used to start gravy or to add to a stock pot.

**Garlic Clove** – Crush the garlic clove with the side of a chef's knife. Take the wide part of the knife and place it on its side (flat surface) over the garlic clove. Hold the knife with one hand, and with the other hand use the side of your fist to pound the garlic. Remove the skin and immediately place it into the sauté pan with olive oil so that the flavor and oils of the garlic immerse into the olive oil.

**Grating** – I am very old fashioned in this sense. When I grate some of my ingredients, I still use a hand grater. There are four sides to a hand grater – two large sides (fine and small circles) and two smaller sides (very fine and wide cuts). There are fine holes, very fine holes, and small circles. For example: Fresh nutmeg nut is grated by using the very fine holes; Asiago, parmesan, or romano cheese are grated by using the fine holes; Fontina and mozzarella cheeses are grated by using the small circles; I use the wide cuts when I shave parmesan cheese for a salad.

**Herbs** – I strongly recommend using fresh herbs. They provide a delicious and robust flavor to dishes. My favorite fresh herbs are nutmeg, basil, rosemary, sage, and tarragon. The leafy herbs, such as basil, rosemary, sage, and tarragon, can be dried, kept in open air, and used for quite some time.

**Lettuce** – When using fresh lettuce of any kind, it should always be washed and dried as much as possible. I do this by separating the leaves and rinsing them under cool water. Then, taking each leaf and patting it dry with a clean, white paper towel. I then tear the leaves instead of cutting them with a knife; then, I put them into the salad or whatever recipe I am making. Wet lettuce can dilute the salad dressing.

**Mirepoix** – Although I do not use this term in any of my recipes, I thought it is a good idea to be familiar with this term. It is a mixture of chopped celery, carrots, and onions. This mixture is the basis of many of my recipes.

**Oven Temperatures** – All of the oven temperatures in my recipes are in Fahrenheit.

**Reduction** – To accomplish this process, increase the heat slightly, then bring the liquid – usually chicken or wine – to a boil, and stir rapidly with a whisk. As the liquid evaporates, it becomes slightly thickened, almost syrupy.

**Sauces or Soups** – Whenever freezing sauces or soups, make sure that you fill the containers up to ½ inch from the top. The freezing process causes the liquid to expand. With soups there is usually a layer of fat that formulates on top. Always scrape this layer of fat from the soup before using.

**Sauté Pan** – Most of my recipes are done in a sauté pan. I usually use a large sauté pan which is about 10 inches in diameter.

**Sea Salt** – I always use sea salt in all of my recipes. I find that sea salt enhances the flavor of a recipe more than any other type of salt.

**Suet** – This is a certain type of fat around the organs of certain types of animals.

**Wine** – I use wine in many of my recipes. I have two favorites that I would like to share with you. The dry, white wine that I like, and strongly recommend, is orvietto. The dry, red wine that I like, and strongly recommend, is chianti.

# Personal Notes